REVISE EDEXCEL GCSE (9—1)
Physical Education
Level 1 / Level 2 Full Course (1PE0) & Short Course (3PE0)

D1454353

REVISION GUIDE

Series Consultant: Harry Smith

Author: Jan Simister

Notes from the publisher

1. In order to ensure that this resource offers high-quality support for the associated Pearson qualification, it has been through a review process by the awarding body. This process confirms that this resource fully covers the teaching and learning content of the specification or part of a specification at which it is aimed. It also confirms that it demonstrates an appropriate balance between the development of subject skills, knowledge and understanding, in addition to preparation for assessment.

Endorsement does not cover any guidance on assessment activities or processes (e.g. practice questions or advice on how to answer assessment questions) included in the resource, nor does it prescribe any particular approach to the teaching or delivery of a related course.

While the publishers have made every attempt to ensure that advice on the qualification and its assessment is accurate, the official specification and associated assessment guidance materials are the only authoritative source of information and should always be referred to for definitive guidance.

Pearson examiners have not contributed to any sections in this resource relevant to examination papers for which they have responsibility.

Examiners will not use endorsed resources as a source of material for any assessment set by Pearson.

Endorsement of a resource does not mean that the resource is required to achieve this Pearson qualification, nor does it mean that it is the only suitable material available to support the qualification, and any resource lists produced by the awarding body shall include this and other appropriate resources.

2. Pearson has robust editorial processes, including answer and fact checks, to ensure the accuracy of the content in this publication, and every effort is made to ensure this publication is free of errors. We are, however, only human, and occasionally errors do occur. Pearson is not liable for any misunderstandings that arise as a result of errors in this publication, but it is our priority to ensure that the content is accurate. If you spot an error, please do contact us at resourcescorrections@pearson.com so we can make sure it is corrected.

Question difficulty
Look at this scale next to each exam-style question. It tells you how difficult the question is.

Contents

Students studying the full course need to study all topics and those studying the short course need to study the topics highlighted.

....
A small bit of small print
Edexcel publishes Sample Assessment Material and the Specification on its website. This is the official content and this book should be used in conjunction with it. The questions in 'Now try this' have been written to help you practise every topic in the book. Remember: the real exam questions may not look like this.

Functions of the skeleton

You need to know the functions of the skeleton and how they apply to physical activity and sport.

Key functions

The functions of the skeleton are:

- production of blood cells
- storage of minerals
- protection of vital organs
- muscle attachment
- formation of joints for movement.

You need to be able to explain how the skeleton carries out all of these functions by giving examples of each in relation to physical activity.

Blood cell production

The following types of blood cell are produced in bone marrow. They are all beneficial to physical performance.

- Platelets help clotting if you are cut.
- Red blood cells transport oxygen to working muscles.
- White blood cells help fight infection.

(For examples of benefits, see page 19.)

Mineral storage

Calcium and phosphorus are stored in bones to help strengthen them.

Protection

Your skeleton provides protection for your vital organs, including the heart.

For example, your skull protects your brain if an opponent follows through wildly with their hockey stick and it hits you on the head during a game.

Golden rule

Always use the phrase **vital organs** and try to give an example to show your understanding.

Aid movement

- The bones provide a place for the muscles to **attach** to, so that when the muscles contract they **pull** the bones to cause movement. Movement occurs at the **joints** of the skeleton.

- Bones also act as **levers**. Levers allow the body to increase the force it can generate or increase the speed of the movement. For example, a tennis player with longer levers will generate more force on a serve. (You can read more about levers on pages 27 and 28.)

Worked example

Which of the following options is correct to complete the sentence below?

The skeletal system protects: **(1 mark)**

☐ **A** Vital organs, for example, bones, muscles, tendons
☒ **B** By providing a hard structure over the organ needing protection
☐ **C** By providing a structure for support
☐ **D** By producing red blood cells which fight disease

Now try this

The skeletal system has several functions. Describe how the skeleton aids movement.   **(2 marks)**

Classification of bones

We classify bones by their shape. Each bone type or classification has a particular function. You need to know the classification type of each bone and its function, and be able to explain the use of each in physical activity.

Long bones

Long bones aid movement by working as levers.

Examples of long bones:

- the humerus
- the femur.

Long bones work as a lever to increase the pace of the ball when kicked.

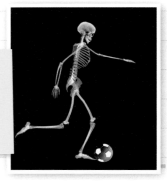

Short bones

Short bones are weight bearing and provide support.

Examples of short bones:

- the carpals
- the tarsals.

Example of use:

- supporting body weight in a handstand.

Flat bones

Flat bones provide protection and a broad surface for muscles to attach to.

Examples of flat bones:

- the cranium
- the ribs
- the scapula.

Example of use:

- the cranium protects the brain if hit by a cricket ball.

Irregular bones

Irregular bones provide protection and a place for muscle attachment.

Example of irregular bones:

- the vertebrae.

Example of use:

- muscles attached to the vertebrae allow a hockey player to bend their back low to dribble a ball.

Vertebrae are irregular bones.

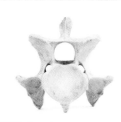

Worked example

Which **type** of bone is the ulna?　　　**(1 mark)**
- ☐ **A** Flat bone
- ☒ **B** Long bone
- ☐ **C** Irregular bone
- ☐ **D** Short bone

If you are not sure, think about where the ulna is. Then think: does it look similar to any bones you know the classification of? Remember that bones are classified by shape; so if it is the same shape as a bone you **do** know, go for that option.

Now try this

Explain how the bone type at the wrist allows the gymnast to perform the position shown.　　　**(3 marks)**

Make sure you identify the bone type you are explaining.

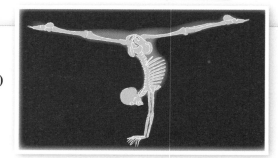

Structure of the skeleton

The skeleton is made up of many bones. Make sure you know the names and locations of the bones below and that you can recognise them on a variety of different diagrams.

Identifying bones

The skeleton provides a framework for muscle attachment, to enable movement for physical activity.

> Remember to look at the shape of the bone to help identify what type it is.

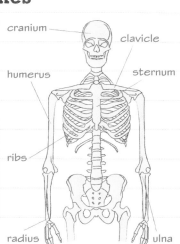

cranium
clavicle
humerus
sternum
ribs
radius
ulna

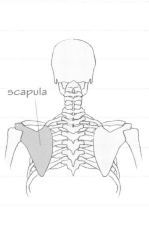

scapula

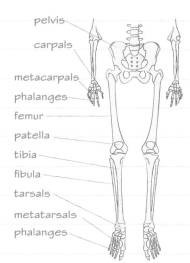

pelvis
carpals
metacarpals
phalanges
femur
patella
tibia
fibula
tarsals
metatarsals
phalanges

The vertebral column has five regions.

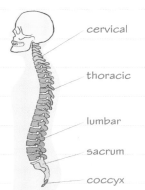

cervical
thoracic
lumbar
sacrum
coccyx

Golden rule

A good way to remember the names and locations of the bones is to practise by labelling blank diagrams of the skeleton.

Worked example

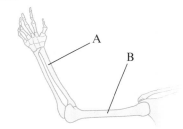

A
B

Identify the bones at A and B.   **(2 marks)**
A: Radius
B: Humerus

> Sometimes it is hard to remember which bone is the radius and which is the ulna. Remember: the radius is the bone that is near the thumb.

Now try this

The rugby player in the image is holding the ball.
State **two** bones located in the hand that help him hold the ball.   **(2 marks)**

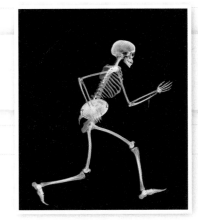

3

Classification of joints

You need to know the names of the bones that form each joint and the range of movement that each joint can do during physical activity.

About joints

- A joint is the place where two or more bones meet. It is where movement can occur.
- Although there are many joints in the human body, you only need to know the joints on this page.
- You should be able to see the similarities between the same types of joints.
- You should be able to give sporting examples of the use of each joint.

Hinge joints

Located at the:

- knee
- elbow
- ankle.

Movement at hinge joints:

- flexion
- extension.

Knee

Golden rule

Remember it is the formation of the joint that dictates the type of movement that can occur there.

Ball and socket joints

Located at the:

- hip
- shoulder.

Movement at ball and socket joints:

- flexion
- extension
- rotation
- circumduction
- abduction
- adduction.

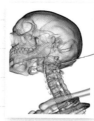
Hip

Pivot joints

Located at the:

- neck (atlas and axis).

Movement at **this** pivot joint:

- rotation.

atlas and axis at the neck

Condyloid joint

Located at the:

- wrist.

Movement at condyloid joints:

- flexion
- extension
- circumduction.

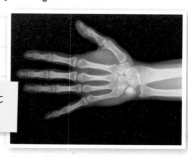
Condyloid joint at the wrist.

Worked example

Which of the following is a movement associated with the pivot joint at the atlas and axis? **(1 mark)**

☐ **A** Adduction
☒ **B** Rotation
☐ **C** Flexion
☐ **D** Extension

Make sure you read the question carefully. This question states 'is associated with' rather than 'is not ...'.

Now try this

What type of joint is formed at the shoulder?

☐ **A** Ball and socket
☐ **B** Ball joint
☐ **C** Dovetail
☐ **D** Hinge

(1 mark)

Movement at joints 1

You need to know the **range of movement** that can be achieved at each of the joints. Flexion and extension can occur at: ball and socket, hinge and condyloid joints.

Joint action: flexion

Flexion is the term given when the angle at a joint **decreases**.

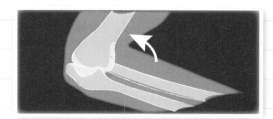

This happens when the bones forming the joint move closer together.

Joint type and application

Flexion occurs at hinge, ball and socket, and condyloid joints.

For example, at the knee when the player is preparing to kick a football.

The lower part of your leg gets closer to the upper part of your leg as the angle at the joint decreases.

Joint action: extension

Extension is the term given when the angle at a joint **increases**.

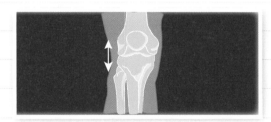

This happens when the bones forming the joint move away from each other.

Joint type and application

Extension occurs at hinge, ball and socket, and condyloid joints.

For example, at the knee when following through after kicking a football.

The lower part of your leg gets further away from the upper part of your leg as the angle at the joint increases.

Worked example

What is the main range of movement possible at the knee joint? **(1 mark)**

The range of movement at the knee joint is flexion to extension.

Flexion and extension could be written in any order but you do need to include both. If a question asks for the range of movement at a joint, you need to put down both parts because the range is the whole movement covered.

Now try this

Identify the joint action necessary to bend the batting (right) arm at the elbow to move into the position shown in the image. **(1 mark)**

This question asks for the joint action. Watch out for the different terms and make sure you are not confusing joint action with joint type or muscle action.

Movement at joints 2

This page covers the joint actions of abduction, adduction and rotation. These movements occur at ball and socket joints.

Joint actions

Abduction = the movement of a limb **away** from the midline of the body.

Adduction = the movement of a limb **towards** the midline of the body.

Rotation = when the bone at a joint moves around its own axis, so making a circular movement.

Rotation allows for the biggest range of movement.

Joint type and application

Abduction occurs at ball and socket joints (hip and shoulder).

For example, at the shoulder when reaching out sideways to intercept a netball. There is abduction at the shoulder.

> To help you remember:
> If something is 'abducted', it is taken away.

Adduction occurs at ball and socket joints (hip and shoulder).

For example, at the hip in the cross-over leg action when throwing a javelin. The leg comes back towards the midline of the body.

> To help you remember:
> Adduction starts with 'add', so it is when a limb is added to the midline of the body.

Rotation occurs at ball and socket joints (hip and shoulder).

For example, at the shoulder when swimming front crawl. The arm rotates around in a circular motion.

Worked example

> Use the image as a guide – it will have been included to help you.

Which of the following is the correct term for the joint action that occurs when the ski jumper takes the skis away from the midline of the body to achieve the position shown in the image? **(1 mark)**

☒ **A** Abduction
☐ **B** Adduction
☐ **C** Flexion
☐ **D** Extension

Now try this

> The word 'range' means you need to include both the start and finish movement for the action identified.

Identify the range of movement at the shoulder during a star jump. **(1 mark)**

Movement at joints 3

In addition to the joint actions on pages 5 and 6, there are three other joint actions you need to know: circumduction, plantar-flexion and dorsi-flexion.

Joint action: circumduction

- Movement in the shape of a cone (conical).
- Allows 360° of movement.
- Occurs at ball and socket joints.
- For example, the shoulder action when swimming butterfly.

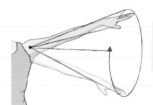

Circumduction at the shoulder.

Joint action: plantar-flexion

- Occurs at the ankle joint.
- Movement of the foot downwards when you point your toes.

Plantar-flexion of the ankle occurs as the gymnast points her toes to make the shape more aesthetically pleasing.

Joint action: dorsi-flexion

- Occurs at the ankle joint.
- Movement of the foot upwards towards the shin (decreasing the angle at the joint).

Dorsi-flexion occurs at the ankle of the leading leg as the athlete jumps the hurdle.

Worked example

State the name of the joint type where circumduction takes place and give an example of its use.   **(2 marks)**

Ball and socket joint. Circling the leg at the hip during a warm up.

Make sure you read the question carefully. This question is asking for the name of a **joint type**, not the name of a **joint**.

Golden rule

Always try to apply your answers to examples in physical activity.

Now try this

Briefly explain how the joint action at the ankle in the image shown assists the volleyball player in their sport.   **(2 marks)**

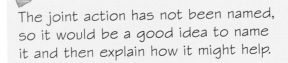

The joint action has not been named, so it would be a good idea to name it and then explain how it might help.

Ligaments, tendons and muscle types

Although bones and muscles are essential for movement, they need help from other structures. These structures work with the bones and muscles to ensure that the body functions well in physical activity.

Ligaments

The role of the ligaments is to join **bone to bone**. Ligaments are formed of tough connective tissue that holds the bones together to form the joint.

Ligaments are relevant to sport and physical activity because they:

- help keep joints stable
- prevent unwanted movement that might cause an injury, such as a dislocation when playing sport.

Tendons

The role of the tendons is to join (skeletal) **muscle to bone**. Tendons are formed of a tough connective tissue.

Tendons are relevant to sport and physical activity because they:

- hold the muscle to the bone, so that when the muscle contracts the muscle can pull on the bone and cause movement at joints.

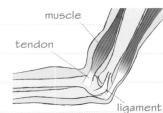

muscle

tendon

ligament

Tendons join muscle to bone and ligaments join bone to bone.

Muscle types

There are three types of muscle. Each muscle type has a different classification based on its characteristics.

Cardiac muscle

- Location: cardiac muscle forms the heart.
- Cardiac muscle is unconsciously controlled – we do not have to think to make it contract.
- For example, cardiac muscle in the heart contracts to pump blood around the body.

Voluntary muscles

- Location: voluntary muscles are the skeletal muscles that attach via tendons to the skeleton to allow movement.
- Voluntary muscles are under conscious control – that is, we move them when we want to; we consciously decide when they should work.
- For example, the biceps contract to flex the arm at the elbow when we perform bicep curls.

Involuntary muscles

- Location: involuntary muscles are found in blood vessels (and the stomach and intestines).
- They contract slowly and rhythmically and are unconsciously controlled – they contract automatically when required to by the body.
- For example, the involuntary muscles in the blood vessels help regulate blood flow for vascular shunting.

Worked example

Which of the following is an example of a voluntary muscle? **(1 mark)**

☒ **A** Deltoid   ☐ **C** Blood vessel

☐ **B** Heart   ☐ **D** Tendon

Notice the word **analyse**. This means you need to really look at each characteristic and see how it links to the particular role of that muscle type.

Now try this

Analyse how the characteristics of voluntary and cardiac muscle types support their function.   **(4 marks)**

Muscles

You need to know the names, location and specific functions of the main muscles that work with the skeleton to produce movement and be able to give examples of their use in sport.

Name: **Deltoid**

Location: Top of the shoulder

Role: Abducts the arm at the shoulder

Example: Lifting your arms above your head to block the ball in volleyball

deltoid

latissimus dorsi

Name: **Latissimus dorsi**

Location: Side of back

Role: Adducts the upper arm at the shoulder / rotates the humerus

Example: Bringing arms back to side during a straight jump in trampolining

> Different types of joint movement plus words to describe the different types of movement at joints, for example, flexion, extension and abduction, are explained on pages 5, 6 and 7.

Name: **Pectoralis major**

Location: Front of upper chest

Role: Adducts the arm at the shoulder

Example: Follow-through from a forehand drive in tennis

pectoralis major

external obliques

Name: **External obliques**

Location: Between lower ribs and abdomen

Role: Rotates the trunk and helps pull chest down

Example: Rotating trunk while throwing the javelin

Worked example

Which one of the following muscles is contracting to allow the tennis player in the image to adduct his arm at the shoulder? **(1 mark)**

☐ **A** Triceps
☐ **B** Latissimus dorsi
☐ **C** Abdominals
☒ **D** Pectoralis major

> If you are not sure, you can move your own body to help you work out which muscles are contracting.

Now try this

Name the movement that occurs when the deltoids contract **and** give an example of its use in a physical activity of your choice. **(2 marks)**

Antagonistic muscle pairs: biceps and triceps

Antagonistic pairs of muscles create opposing movement at joints. You need to know the **four** different pairs covered on the following pages and relate them to sporting techniques.

Antagonistic pairs

Skeletal muscles work together to provide movement of the joints.

While one muscle **contracts**, another **relaxes** to create movement.

Muscles working together like this are called **antagonistic pairs**.

The muscle contracting is the **agonist** (prime mover).

The muscle relaxing is the **antagonist**.

Remember, muscles are connected to bones via tendons. When the muscles contract, they pull on the tendon which pulls on the bone. This creates the movement.

Biceps and triceps

These two muscles are an example of an antagonistic muscle pair.

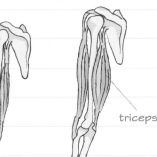

Name: **Biceps**

Location: Front of upper arm

Role: Flexion of the arm at the elbow

Example: Upwards phase of a biceps curl

biceps

triceps

Name: **Triceps**

Location: Back of upper arm

Role: Extension of the arm at the elbow

Example: Straightening the arms in a chest press

During this part of the movement, the triceps is the antagonist – it is relaxing to allow the biceps to contract.

During this movement, the biceps is the antagonist – it is relaxing to allow the triceps to contract.

Worked example

Explain the term 'antagonistic pair' in relation to muscle movement.   **(1 mark)**

One muscle contracts while the other relaxes to bring about movement.

EXAM ALERT!

Explain the role of **each** muscle in the antagonistic pair.

Now try this

Complete the blanks by identifying the muscles involved in the movement described.   **(2 marks)**
The .... is the agonist when the goalkeeper extends his arm at the elbow and the .... is the antagonist.

Antagonistic muscle pairs: quadriceps and hamstrings

You need to know which muscles work together to bring about movement and use this knowledge to analyse sporting actions.

The quadriceps and hamstrings are an antagonistic muscle pair.

Name:	**Quadriceps**		Name:	**Hamstrings**
Location:	Front of upper leg		Location:	Back of upper leg
Role:	Extension of the leg at the knee		Role:	Flexion of the leg at the knee
Example:	Straightening the leading leg going over a hurdle		Example:	Bending the trailing leg going over a hurdle

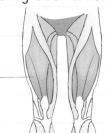

quadriceps

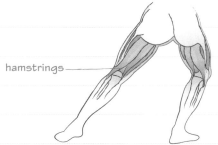

hamstrings

During this part of the movement the hamstrings act as the antagonist. It is relaxing to allow the quadriceps to contract.

During this part of the movement the quadriceps is the antagonist. It is relaxing to allow the hamstrings to contract.

The quadriceps and hamstrings work together so the performer can clear the hurdle.

Golden rules

- If you are not sure of the correct spelling of muscle names, write them like they sound.
- Always write the name in full, for example, quadriceps, not quads.

Worked example

Which one of the following muscles is contracting to allow the cyclist in the image to flex her leg at the knee? **(1 mark)**

☐ **A** Latissimus dorsi
☒ **B** Hamstrings
☐ **C** Gastrocnemius
☐ **D** Quadriceps

EXAM ALERT!

Make sure you know the actions of the muscles. Questions often have a picture to help you visualise the movement.

Now try this

Name the antagonist that is relaxing to allow the cyclist in the image above to flex her leg at the knee. **(1 mark)**

Antagonistic muscle pairs: gastrocnemius and tibialis anterior

Make sure you know the names and locations of these muscles and can give an example of their use.

Name: **Gastrocnemius**

Location: Back of lower leg

Role: Plantar-flexion at the ankle

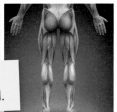

The **gastrocnemius** muscles are highlighted.

Example: Pointing the toes when performing a pike jump in trampolining

> ### Golden rule
> Always use the correct name for the gastrocnemius, not the calf. Also remember it has a 'C' sound in it (gast-ro-C-nemius).

Name: **Tibialis anterior**

Location: Front of lower leg

Role: Dorsi-flexion at the ankle

The **tibialis anterior** muscles are highlighted.

Example: Bringing the toes up towards the shins when extending the legs in the long jump

Which action is plantar-flexion?

To help you recall which action is plantar-flexion, remember:

Pointing toes starts with the letter **P** and so does the action **p**lantar-flexion.

Where is the tibialis anterior?

To help you recall where the tibialis anterior muscle is located, remember:

- the word 'anterior' means front
- the word 'tibialis' starts with the name of the bone – the tibia
- the muscle is located on the front of the tibia.

Worked example

What term is being described below?
When two muscles work together, one muscle starts to contract to pull the bone, the other starts to relax to aid the movement. **(1 mark)**

Antagonistic pair

> ### Golden rule
> When asked to give an example, always use the most obvious example to make sure it is correct, rather than giving a more obscure answer.

Now try this

Double check if a question is asking for the agonist or the antagonist.

Name the antagonist supporting the agonist to allow the gymnast to point his toes. **(1 mark)**

Antagonistic muscle pairs: hip flexors and gluteus maximus

Make sure you know the names and locations of these muscles and can give an example of their use.

Name: **Hip flexors**
Location: Very top of front of upper leg
Role: Flexion of leg at the hip

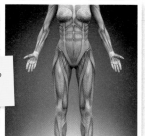

The **hip flexor** muscles are highlighted.

Example: Bringing the legs up in a seat-drop in trampolining

Name: **Gluteus maximus**
Location: Buttocks
Role: Extension of the leg at the hip

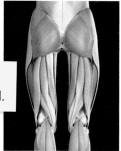

The **gluteus maximus** muscles are highlighted.

Example: Lifting the leg back at the hip when running

Example of hip flexion in diving.

Golden rules

Notice the words **flexion** and **extension** are used for the action at the hip as well as the knee. The same rules apply.

- Flexion occurs when the angle at the joint gets smaller.
- Extension occurs when the angle at the joint gets bigger.

Example of hip extension in basketball.

Worked example

Which **one** of the following muscles is contracting to allow the footballer in the image to extend her leg at the hip?   **(1 mark)**

☒ **A** Gluteus maximus
☐ **B** Hamstrings
☐ **C** Abdominals
☐ **D** Quadriceps

Note that the question refers to the hip, not the knee, and asks about extension rather than flexion.

Now try this

Name the agonist that brings the knees up to the chest in a tuck jump and identify the joint action occurring at the hip.

(2 marks)

13

Muscle fibre types

Muscle fibres types fall into three main categories. You need to know the differences between the types of muscle fibre and how each is used in performance.

Types of skeletal muscle

Skeletal muscles are made up of different muscle fibres. Muscle fibres are either **fast twitch** or **slow twitch**.

There is one type of slow twitch fibre: type I.

There are two types of fast twitch fibre: type IIa and type IIx.

The different types of muscle fibre have different capabilities and are recruited depending on the task required.

Each type has its advantages (👍) and disadvantages (👎).

Slow twitch type I

- Produce low force.
- Slow speed of contraction.
- High endurance.

👍 Good in endurance activities to keep going without tiring – for example, leg muscles in a cross-country race.

👎 Do not produce much power.

Fast twitch type IIa

- Produce high force.
- Moderate speed of contraction.
- Medium endurance.

👍 More resistant to fatigue than type IIx – for example, in a 400-metre sprint.

👎 Not as powerful as type IIx or as resistant to fatigue as type I.

Golden rule

You should always be clear if you are referring to type IIa or type IIx fast twitch fibres.

Fast twitch type IIx

- Produce very high force.
- Fast contracting.
- Low endurance.

👍 Good for short, explosive actions requiring power, strength and speed – for example, a sprint start or a 100-metre sprint.

👎 Only provide power for a very short time before becoming fatigued.

Summary of characteristics

	Slow twitch type 1	Fast twitch type IIa	Fast twitch type IIx
Force of contraction	low	high	very high
Speed of concentration	slow	medium	fast
Resistance to fatigue	high	moderate	low
Aerobic or anaerobic	aerobic	aerobic and anaerobic	anaerobic
Myoglobin	high	medium	low
Mitochondria	high	medium	low
Capillary network	good	moderate	low

Worked example

Name the muscle fibre type that is predominantly used when constantly running throughout a game to mark your opponent in football.   **(1 mark)**

Slow twitch type I

Look for the key words 'constantly' and 'throughout' in the question help to show that it is an endurance requirement.

Now try this

Describe a characteristic of type IIx muscle fibres and how it is an advantage to a basketball performer.   **(2 marks)**

Remember: 'characteristic' means a quality or feature that specifically belongs to the item.

Cardiovascular system 1

You need to know the **functions** of the cardiovascular system, what it does and how this is relevant to physical performance.

The cardiovascular system

The cardiovascular system consists of:

- **the blood** – the medium that the gases, blood cells and nutrients are transported in
- **the blood vessels** – the structures that carry the blood
- **the heart** – which circulates blood around the body by squeezing blood out to the blood vessels each time it beats.

Transport of oxygen

The cardiovascular system transports **oxygen** around the body in the blood. It carries oxygen **to** the muscles and vital organs. Oxygen is needed in energy production for physical activity.

Transport of carbon dioxide

Carbon dioxide is produced as a by-product during energy production. The cardiovascular system takes carbon dioxide **away** from the muscles to get rid of it from the body.

Transport of nutrients

Nutrients are broken down from the food we eat and transported to the body in the blood.

Athletes need macro- and micronutrients in order to perform well. (These are covered on pages 91 and 92.)

Clotting of open wounds

Platelets that are transported in the blood help to clot wounds by gathering at the site and forming a plug to prevent blood loss.

Clotting of blood is needed, for example, if a performer falls and grazes their knee, so that they can stay on the field of play.

Regulation of body temperature

We get hot when we do physical activity because heat is a by-product of energy production.

We can also get cold doing physical activity outside in low temperatures.

The body attempts to keep a constant temperature.

Physical activity causes changes in **body temperature**.

When the body temperature rises:

- the blood vessels under the skin increase in diameter (**vasodilation**) to increase blood flow to the capillaries under the surface of the skin so heat can radiate from the skin.

When body temperature drops:

- the blood vessels under the skin decrease in diameter (**vasoconstriction**) to decrease blood flow to the capillaries under the surface of the skin so less heat is lost by radiation.

 Worked example

Which of the following is a function of the cardiovascular system?   **(1 mark)**

☐ **A** Breathing in air containing oxygen
☒ **B** Regulating body temperature
☐ **C** Protection and muscle attachment
☐ **D** Breathing out air containing carbon dioxide

Note the question refers to the cardiovascular system and **not** the respiratory system.

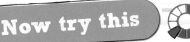 **Now try this**

Explain how the cardiovascular system helps regulate body temperature when the skier starts to get cold.

(2 marks)

Cardiovascular system 2

You need to know the structure of the cardiovascular system. Make sure you know the names and location of the components and their role in maintaining blood circulation during physical activity.

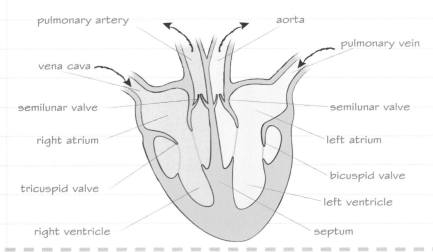

pulmonary artery   aorta
pulmonary vein
vena cava
semilunar valve   semilunar valve
right atrium   left atrium
bicuspid valve
tricuspid valve   left ventricle
right ventricle   septum

Golden rule

When looking at a diagram of the heart remember that it is a cross-section, viewed from the front. This is why the right-hand side is actually on the left of the diagram! Imagine your heart to check the sides.

- **Tricuspid valve** is on the **right** side of the heart between the right atrium and the right ventricle.
- **Bicuspid valve** is on the **left** side of the heart between the left atrium and left ventricle.
- **Semilunar valves** are between the ventricles and the pulmonary artery and vein.

Valves help keep the blood moving forward by shutting behind blood that has passed through, to prevent it from flowing back the way it came.

- **Vena cava** is the main **vein** bringing deoxygenated blood back **to** the heart so it can be pumped to the lungs to collect oxygen.
- **Aorta** is the main **artery** and carries oxygenated blood **away** from the left ventricle to take oxygen to the working muscles.
- **Pulmonary artery** receives deoxygenated blood from the right ventricle to take to the lungs to receive oxygen.
- **Pulmonary vein** brings oxygenated blood from the lungs to the left atrium.

- **Right atrium** receives deoxygenated blood from the body via the vena cava.
- **Left atrium** receives oxygenated blood from the lungs via the pulmonary vein.
- **Right ventricle** receives deoxygenated blood from the **right** atrium via the tricuspid value.
- **Left ventricle** receives oxygenated blood from the **left** atrium via the bicuspid valve.
- **Septum** is the wall that separates the left and right sides of the heart.

Worked example

Explain the function of the pulmonary artery. **(2 marks)**

The pulmonary artery carries deoxygenated blood from the heart to the lungs **so** the blood can get oxygen, which is eventually pumped to the working muscles.

Knowledge – say what you know.
Application – apply it. Use linking words such as 'so', 'meaning that' and 'therefore' so the knowledge leads on to the application.

Now try this

Complete the diagram to show the missing components assisting the flow of deoxygenated blood to the lungs.

(2 marks)

| Vena cava | → | | → | Tricuspid valve | → | Right ventricle | → | | → | Pulmonary artery |

Blood vessels

You need to know both the structure and function of the blood vessels and how this is relevant in terms of blood pressure, oxygenated blood, deoxygenated blood and response to physical exercise.

Arteries

Structure

- Thick muscular and elastic walls.
- Small internal diameter (lumen).

Functions

- Carry blood at high pressure **away** from the heart.
- Mainly carry oxygenated blood (exception: pulmonary artery carries deoxygenated blood to lungs from heart).

Relevance

Blood pressure increases during exercise as the working muscles demand more oxygen, increasing blood flow. The muscles in the artery walls contract and relax automatically. When the muscle relaxes, the arteries dilate so there is more room for the blood to travel through, helping regulate blood pressure.

Capillaries

Structure

- Very thin walls (only one-cell thick).
- Small internal diameter.

Functions

- Link smaller arteries with smaller veins.
- Carry blood at very low pressure.

Relevance

Allow **gaseous exchange**. Walls are very thin to allow gases and nutrients to pass through them, therefore getting oxygen to the muscles and removing carbon dioxide.

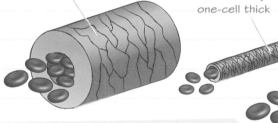

Arteries have thick muscular walls

Capillaries are very narrow and have very thin walls that are only one-cell thick

Veins have thin walls

The differences between arteries, capillaries and veins.

Golden rule

Remember: All arteries carry blood **away** from the heart and all veins carry blood **towards** the heart.

Veins

Structure

- Thin walls.
- Large internal diameter.
- Contain valves.

Functions

- Carry blood at low pressure towards heart.
- Mainly carry deoxygenated blood (exception: pulmonary vein carries oxygenated blood from lungs to heart).

Relevance

Veins carry deoxygenated blood from the muscles. The wide internal diameter allows blood to pass through more easily and the valves help return the blood to the heart by preventing backflow due to low pressure.

Worked example

Which one of the following is a characteristic of capillaries?   **(1 mark)**

☐ **A** Has valves
☐ **B** Thick muscular wall
☒ **C** One-cell thick
☐ **D** Carries blood under high pressure

Think about the function of capillaries. The capillaries need to be thin to allow the gases to move in and out of them easily.

Now try this

State the type of blood vessel that holds blood at high pressure.   **(1 mark)**

Vascular shunting

You need to be able to explain the redistribution of blood flow (**vascular shunting**) during exercise compared to at rest.

Vascular shunting

When you exercise your working muscles need more oxygen. Oxygen is attached to the red blood cells in the blood and carried to your active muscles.

Your heart rate and stroke volume (see page 26) increase so more blood is circulating every minute.

Blood is diverted away from inactive areas to the working muscles. This is called **vascular shunting**.

Blood can be shunted away from the stomach. This is why it is important that digestion is complete before exercise begins.

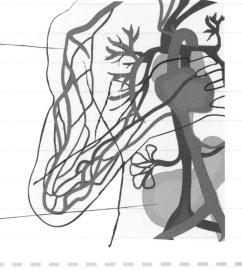

Vasoconstriction

- Vasoconstriction means that the blood vessels are constricted (squeezed) to make them smaller.
- When you start to exercise, chemical changes trigger signals from your nervous system.
- These signals cause the blood vessels that supply the **inactive** areas (for example, the digestive system) to **constrict**, reducing blood flow to these areas.

Vasodilation

- Vasodilation means that the blood vessels are dilated to make them bigger.
- When you start to exercise, chemical changes trigger signals from your nervous system.
- These signals cause the blood vessels that supply the **active** areas (the working muscles) to **dilate**, increasing blood flow to these areas. This means that these muscles receive more oxygen and nutrients.

Worked example

You could use alternative words to 'greater' and 'lower', such as 'more' or 'less', but always re-read your answer to make sure the meaning is clear.

Using the words in the table below, complete the following statements about blood flow whilst at rest and during physical activity.

unchanged	equal
lower	greater

Blood flow to the digestive system is ......*greater*...... at rest than when exercising. **(1 mark)**
Blood flow to the muscular system is ......*lower*...... at rest than when exercising. **(1 mark)**

Now try this

Using the words in the table below, complete the statements that follow.

vascular shunting	digestion
cardiac output	increased blood flow

Reduced blood flow to specific areas of the body is achieved through ....
There is a need for .... to the muscles during exercise. **(2 marks)**

Plasma, platelets and blood cells

You need to know the function and importance of red and white blood cells, platelets and plasma for physical activity and sport.

The four main components of blood

The four main components of the blood each play a role in enabling physical activity to take place.

Plasma

Plasma transports the blood cells, platelets and nutrients to the different parts of the body.

Plasma is the liquid part of blood.

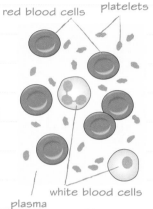

red blood cells   platelets

white blood cells

plasma

Red blood cells

Red blood cells carry oxygen and remove carbon dioxide.

- Oxygen is diffused into the bloodstream from the alveoli in the lungs.
- The oxygen then binds (joins) with the haemoglobin in the red blood cells and is transported (by the plasma) to the working muscles where it is needed for any aerobic activity.
- Some of the carbon dioxide produced in the tissue is transported away from the muscles. It can be either attached to red blood cells or just carried in the plasma.

Platelets

Platelets help prevent bleeding as they can stick to each other and to the walls of the blood vessels. If a performer gets cut while playing, the platelets flowing in the plasma stick together and form a plug to prevent further blood loss.

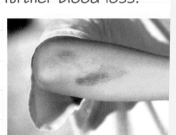

If cut, a performer is not allowed to continue playing until the bleeding has stopped.

White blood cells

White blood cells help fight infection. They travel around the body in the plasma and fight any infections or diseases that may be there.

Performers need to stay free from illness so they can continue to train and maintain their performance level.

Golden rule

Always try to apply the topic to physical activity.

 Worked example

Explain why plasma is so important to sports performance.   **(3 marks)**

Plasma is the liquid component of the blood.

Because it is liquid it flows through the blood vessels, allowing transportation of anything within it.

Therefore plasma can carry red blood cells within it, supplying oxygen to the working muscles for physical activity.

Generally when answering 'explain' questions you need to **show your knowledge** and either **apply or justify** the point you are making. Remember, if the question asks you to **explain** you need to include a **justification** or **reason** to support the initial point too.
Knowledge (what is it?)
Application (what is the impact?)
Justification (why is it important?)

 Now try this

State the component of blood responsible for fighting infection.   **(1 mark)**

Composition of air

You need to know the composition of inhaled and exhaled air and the impact of physical activity and sport on this composition.

Inhaled air

Inhaled air is the air we breathe **in** to the lungs.

The percentages of the gases in inhaled air are shown in the table below.

Nitrogen	78%
Oxygen	21%
Carbon dioxide	0.04%

Exhaled air

Exhaled air is the air we breathe **out** of the lungs.

The percentages of the gases in exhaled air are shown in the table below.

Nitrogen	78%
Oxygen	16%
Carbon dioxide	4%

The differences between inhaled and exhaled air

How do the percentages of the different gases vary between inhaled and exhaled air?

- Nitrogen has remained the same.
- Oxygen levels have gone down.
- Carbon dioxide levels have risen.

You need to be able to account for these changes.

Remember: the reason these three gases do not add up to 100% is due to the rest of the air being made up of tiny percentages of other gases. You do not need to know these other gases for your exam.

Nitrogen

- The largest percentage of gas.
- The same amount is breathed out as is breathed in.
- Does not go down as the body does not use it during physical activity.
- Does not go up as the body does not produce it during physical activity.

Oxygen

- Levels decrease as oxygen is used in energy production for activity or for recovery, so there is less oxygen to breathe out.

Carbon dioxide

- Levels increase as carbon dioxide is produced as a by-product of energy production.

Worked example

The chart below represents the three main gases found in exhaled air.

Identify the gases labelled A and B.   **(2 marks)**

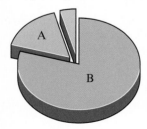

A = oxygen
B = nitrogen

Use of data

Think about the percentages of the gases and relate them to the pie chart. Which gas forms the highest percentage of air?

In this example it does not make a difference that the question refers to exhaled air, as the changes do not affect the proportions of the gases.

Now try this

State **two** reasons why the level of nitrogen remains the same in inhaled and exhaled air.   **(2 marks)**

Lung volumes

Make sure you know the difference between tidal volume and vital capacity, as well as the reasons for changes to tidal volume as a result of participation in physical activity and sport.

Lung volume and tidal volume

Lung volume refers to the capacity of the lungs (how much air they can hold). The greater the volume of the lungs, the more air they can hold.

Tidal volume is the amount of air inspired (inhaled) or expired (exhaled) in a normal breath.

When our bodies are at rest, breathing is slower and shallower than when exercising. This is because the demand for energy is less, so:

- less air containing oxygen needs to be breathed in
- less carbon dioxide needs to be breathed out (as less is produced by the body).

Changes to tidal volume on a graph

The lines on the graph show tidal volume at rest and during exercise.

Tidal volume at rest

- These lines represent the depth of breathing; at rest their maximum value is 0.5 litres. If you take 12 breaths a minute this means your lungs will take in 6 litres of air per minute. This provides enough oxygen for energy requirements at rest.

Tidal volume during exercise

- These lines show the increased depth of breathing as a result of exercise. The graph shows an increase from 0.5 to 2.5 litres.
- Breathing rate will also increase.
- This increase in tidal volume and breathing rate means you can breathe as much as 150 litres of air per minute during exercise.

Vital capacity is the maximum amount of air the lungs can expire (breathe out) after the maximum amount they can inspire (breathe in).

Vital capacity is made up of:

- tidal volume
- expiratory reserve volume – the maximum volume that can be exhaled
- inspiratory reserve volume – the maximum volume that can be inhaled.

Changes to tidal volume during exercise

During exercise you need to increase airflow into and out of your lungs. This is because:

- you need to get more oxygen into your lungs so it can diffuse into the bloodstream for additional energy production
- you need to breathe out the additional carbon dioxide produced during exercise.

By breathing more deeply when you exercise you:

- inhale more oxygen
- exhale more carbon dioxide.

To allow this to happen, tidal volume will increase.

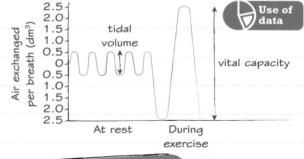

Changes in tidal volume at rest and during exercise.

Which **one** of the following describes tidal volume?   **(1 mark)**
☐ A The maximum amount of air expired
☐ B The total amount of all lung volumes
☒ C The normal amount of air inspired at rest
☐ D The maximum amount of air inspired

Remember to eliminate the options that are definitely incorrect first.

During exercise tidal volume will increase, becoming nearer to the lungs' vital capacity. Define the term vital capacity.   **(1 mark)**

The respiratory system

You need to know the location of the main components of the respiratory system and their role in the movement of oxygen and carbon dioxide into and out of the body.

Lungs

- There are two lungs (left and right).
- The lungs allow the movement of air in and out of the body (ventilation).
- Air enters the lungs during inspiration (the process of breathing in).
- Air leaves the lungs during expiration (the process of breathing out).

lungs

alveoli

bronchi

diaphragm

bronchioles

The respiratory system is made up of many components. You only need to know the ones shown in the diagram.

Bronchi and bronchioles

- The air travels to each of the lungs via the **bronchi** – the term for both the left and right bronchus that take air to each of the lungs.
- The passages that the air travels down get smaller as the bronchi subdivide. The smaller airways from the bronchi are called **bronchioles**.
- Bronchioles branch out throughout the lungs and carry the air from the bronchi to the **alveoli**.

Alveoli

- The alveoli are tiny air sacs.
- They are attached to the branches of the bronchioles throughout the lungs.
- At the alveoli the exchange of oxygen and carbon dioxide occurs (see page 23).

There are millions of alveoli in the lungs.

Diaphragm

- **During inspiration** the diaphragm contracts and flattens to make more space in the chest so the lungs can expand to pull in air.
- **During expiration** the diaphragm relaxes and returns to a dome shape, making the chest cavity smaller. This helps force the air out of the lungs.

Due to the demand for additional oxygen by the working muscles during exercise, the **rate** and **depth** of breathing increase. This enables carbon dioxide to be removed at a faster rate.

Worked example

Explain the role of the diaphragm during inspiration.   **(3 marks)**

The diaphragm contracts and flattens to make more room for the lungs to expand into, so that more air can be taken into the body. The increase in space helps to draw the air in from the atmosphere to the lungs.

Now try this

Which of the following is **not** a function of the respiratory system?   **(1 mark)**

☐ **A** Inspiration

☐ **B** Blood transportation

☐ **C** Gaseous exchange

☐ **D** Expiration

EXAM ALERT!

Questions referring to the **respiratory** system are just about the process and mechanics of breathing and gas exchange.

Questions about the **cardio-respiratory** system are about **both** the respiratory **and** the cardiovascular system. Mark sure you read the question carefully.

The alveoli and gas exchange

You need to know how the structure of the alveoli enables gas exchange, as well as the process of gas exchange to meet the demands of varying intensities of exercise.

Gas exchange

Gases move from areas of high concentration to areas of low concentration.

Think about a fizzy drink. When you first open a bottle there are lots of bubbles of carbon dioxide (CO_2), which leave the liquid to join the air. This is because there is a high concentration of CO_2 inside the bottle compared to outside the bottle. This is why the drink will go flat if the lid is left off the bottle.

The same happens at the alveoli as happens to the bottle of fizzy drink.

Structure of alveoli

- Very tiny air sacs.
- Very thin walls.
- Surrounded by capillaries.

Gas exchange – alveoli to capillaries

- Alveoli – high pressure/concentration of oxygen.
- Capillaries surrounding alveoli (from muscles) – low pressure/concentration of oxygen.
- Movement of oxygen from high pressure to low through thin walls of capillaries and alveoli.
- Capillaries gain oxygen from the alveoli and transport it around the body.

Gas exchange – capillaries to alveoli

The reverse happens with the movement of carbon dioxide.

- Capillaries surrounding alveoli (from muscles) – high pressure/concentration of CO_2.
- Alveoli – low pressure/concentration of CO_2.
- Movement of CO_2 from high pressure to low.
- CO_2 is moved out of the blood into the alveoli to be breathed out.

Gas exchange occurs between the alveoli and the capillaries, and between the capillaries and the muscle tissue.

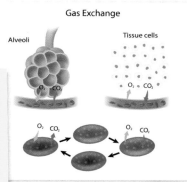

Gas Exchange

Alveoli   Tissue cells

Exercise intensities

Gas exchange varies with the intensity of exercise.

- During aerobic activity there is an increase in breathing rate and an increase in gas exchange to meet the demands of the working muscles for more oxygen.
- After anaerobic activity there is an elevated breathing rate, allowing greater gas exchange to aid recovery.

Worked example

Explain one reason why carbon dioxide can diffuse from a capillary to the alveoli.   **(2 marks)**

There will be high levels of carbon dioxide in the capillaries and lower levels in the alveoli, **therefore** the carbon dioxide will move from high pressure in the capillaries to the alveoli to try to even out the concentration of CO_2.

Although the question asks for only one reason, 2 marks are available – so make sure you link the parts of your answer.

Now try this

(a) What will the concentration of oxygen in the blood be just after it leaves the alveoli?

(b) Give a reason for your answer to (a).

(2 marks)

Energy and energy sources

You need to know about aerobic and anaerobic energy production and their use in different physical activities and sport.

Energy production

Aerobic exercise **uses oxygen** for energy production. (This is aerobic respiration, not to be confused with breathing.)

Activities using aerobic respiration are:

- long duration
- moderate pace rather than intense pace.

One example is long-distance running.

Anaerobic exercise **does not use oxygen** in energy production.

Activities using anaerobic respiration are:

- high intensity
- very short duration.

One example is elite 100-metre sprinting or explosive activities, such as shot put.

Energy sources

Fats are an energy source for aerobic activity.

They:

- require oxygen to break down into glucose
- are slow to break down
- once broken down give large quantities of energy for exercise.

Carbohydrates are an energy source for aerobic **and** anaerobic activity. They:

- do not require oxygen to break down into glucose
- do not give as much energy as fats
- are easier to break down therefore release energy more quickly than fats.

Aerobic energy equation

$$GLUCOSE + O_2 \rightarrow CO_2 + H_2O + HEAT + ENERGY$$

Key

O_2 = oxygen CO_2 = carbon dioxide
H_2O = water

This equation means:

- you use glucose and oxygen to release energy aerobically
- the process produces carbon dioxide, water and heat in addition to energy.

Lactic acid

Lactic acid is produced as a by-product when carbohydrates are broken down without oxygen during anaerobic respiration.

$$GLUCOSE \rightarrow LACTIC\ ACID + ENERGY$$

Without oxygen, lactic acid will accumulate (build up) in the blood and muscle tissue, causing muscles to become tired and work less efficiently, causing a drop in performance.

Worked example

Why do carbon dioxide levels increase during aerobic respiration?   **(1 mark)**

They increase because CO_2 is produced during aerobic respiration.

This is a straightforward question. Say what you know about carbon dioxide.

Key terms

- **Respiration** – the process of energy production.
- **Energy sources** – the macronutrients that provide energy.

Now try this

Explain why a 1500-metre runner cannot maintain the same speed over 1500 metres as a sprinter can over 400 metres.   **(4 marks)**

 You need to think about the intensity of the activities and different types of respiration to help you answer this question.

24

Short-term effects of exercise on the muscular system

Short-term effects of exercise are the ways your body responds as soon as it starts to exercise or, if exercising, how it responds to an increase in intensity of exercise. These changes happen so that the body can meet the increased demands due to the exercise undertaken.

As you start to exercise there is an increased demand for energy. This energy can be supplied through aerobic or anaerobic respiration.

In most sports you will work as hard as you can at some point, for example, sprinting for a ball. This requires anaerobic energy production.

Anaerobic energy production can lead to:

- **muscle fatigue** due to the increased acidity in the cells as a result of the reactions taking place to release the required energy
- **lactate accumulation** in the muscle tissue and bloodstream due to lack of oxygen.

During recovery when oxygen is available, lactate can be broken down and removed from the body and some can be converted back into energy for physical work.

When you start to exercise the muscles require energy quickly. They use:

- the oxygen stores in the muscles (myoglobin)
- the haemoglobin in the blood.

However, there is still not enough oxygen to work aerobically for long. This results in an **oxygen deficit** where the muscles produce energy anaerobically.

During recovery 'extra' oxygen is required (above that normally used at rest). The extra oxygen is needed to:

- replenish myoglobin stores with oxygen
- break down lactate or lactic acid into carbon dioxide and water
- allow energy stores in the muscles to be replenished.

Key terms

- **Muscle fatigue** – when the efficiency of the muscles drops, reducing the level of performance.
- **Lactate** – a chemical formed through anaerobic respiration.
- **Lactate accumulation** – when the levels of lactate (a by-product of anaerobic respiration) start to build up in the muscle tissue or blood.

Relevance to performer

Muscle fatigue occurs because the muscle is not able to produce the energy it needs for the level of activity, due to an increase in acidity in the muscle cells. This increased level of acidity interrupts the normal process of energy production, meaning that the muscles have to reduce the intensity they are working at to allow the muscles time to recover.

Remember, you do not need to learn definitions word for word, but they must express the correct meaning. Make sure you give the meaning of both 'lactate' and 'accumulation'.

Worked example

How would muscle fatigue affect the following players?
- A footballer
- A 1500-metre runner   **(2 marks)**

A footballer would not be able to keep up with the pace of the game, losing their opponent, therefore reducing their contribution to the game. A 1500-metre runner would not be able to run as fast in the final laps and would therefore record a slower time. Muscle fatigue has a detrimental effect on any performance.

Now try this

Define the term lactate accumulation.   **(2 marks)**

Short-term effects of exercise on the cardio-respiratory system

Short-term effects of exercise are the ways your body responds as soon as it starts to exercise.

Cardiovascular system

When you start to exercise there is an increase in:

- heart rate (HR)
- stroke volume (SV)
- blood pressure
- cardiac output (as HR × SV = cardiac output).

Vascular shunting will also occur.

After exercise the cardio-respiratory system will slowly return to its resting values.

Respiratory system

Physical activity initiates an increase in:

- depth of breathing
- rate of breathing
- gas exchange

and therefore:

- tidal volume.

Oxygen deficit will also occur, depending on the nature of the exercise.

These changes mean the respiratory and cardiovascular systems work together to help the performer meet the increased demands of exercise.

- As the breathing depth and rate increases it draws air in to the body faster.
- Gas exchange can occur more quickly, and the increase in blood flow (due to increased heart rate and stroke volume) means that the blood can pick up more oxygen from the lungs and transport it more quickly to the muscles.
- There is increased oxygen delivery to the muscles from the lungs and increased removal of carbon dioxide from the muscles to the lungs.

Key terms

- **Heart rate** (HR) – the number of times the heart beats per minute.
- **Stroke volume** (SV) – the amount of blood leaving the heart each beat.
- **Cardiac output** – HR × SV, the amount of blood leaving the heart per minute.
- **Breathing rate** – the number of breaths per minute.
- **Recovery rate** – the time it takes for heart rate to return to resting rate.

Use the information you are given:
HR × SV = cardiac output

Worked example

Analyse the graph to determine the effect of exercise on cardiac output. **(3 marks)**

The graph shows an increase in heart rate and stroke volume. As heart rate multiplied by stroke volume equals cardiac output, if they have both increased cardiac output must also increase as a result of exercise.

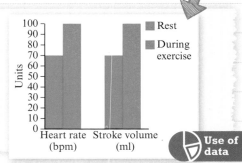

Use of data

Now try this

Use the information in the graph to guide you.

(a) Which student had the lowest resting heart rate? **(1 mark)**
(b) Whose pulse rate increased the most during exercise? **(1 mark)**
(c) Which student recovered from exercise the quickest? **(1 mark)**

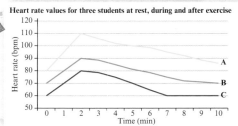

Heart rate values for three students at rest, during and after exercise

Lever systems 1

Lever systems help you to move. They can increase the amount you can lift or increase the speed at which you can move something. You need to be able to correctly sketch and label the three classes of lever and give examples of their use in sport.

Levers and lever systems

A lever is a rigid bar that rotates around a fulcrum to apply a force to a load.

Within in the body:

- the **lever** is a bone
- the **fulcrum** (or pivot) is a joint
- the **effort** (or force) is provided by muscles
- the weight of the body part or object being moved is the **load**.

There are also levers outside of the body, for example, a racket used to apply force to a ball.

There are three classes of lever system. Each class has the same components but they are arranged in a different order.

The same shape is always used to represent each component of a lever system.

The fulcrum is shown as a triangle.

The effort is an arrow (pointing in the direction that the effort is applied).

The load is a square.

The lever a straight line. ————

The order of the components determines the class of lever.

First class lever system

The fulcrum is between the load and the effort.

In this attacking header, the head coming down on the ball is the **load**, the **fulcrum** is the atlas and axis joint, and the muscles allowing the head to move in this way provide the **effort**.

First class lever – extending the arm at the elbow.

Extending the arm at the elbow is another first class lever. This is because the triceps muscle attaches to the ulna at the elbow, to provide the effort. The fulcrum (the elbow) is in the centre of the lever system.

Second class lever system

The load is between the effort and the fulcrum.

During calf raises, the ball of the foot is the **fulcrum**; the gastrocnemius provides the **effort** to lift the whole body weight, and the weights being held are the **load**.

Worked example

What component of a lever system is represented by a triangle? **(1 mark)**

☒ **A** Fulcrum   ☐ **C** Effort
☐ **B** Lever   ☐ **D** Load

You will need to learn these symbols so you can sketch the lever systems.

Now try this

(a) Using the symbols on the image as a guide, identify the lever system being used by the rower.

(b) Give a reason for your choice. **(2 marks)**

Lever systems 2

Lever systems provide a mechanical advantage or disadvantage. You will need to know the difference between these terms, the mechanical advantage or disadvantage that different classes of levers provide, and the impact on sporting performance.

Third class lever

The effort is between the load and the fulcrum.

Third class levers are the most common lever systems in the human body.

An example of a third class lever is a biceps curl. The fulcrum is the elbow joint, the load is the weight being lifted, and the effort is provided by the biceps pulling the lever (the bone) to lift the weight.

Third class lever – biceps curl.

Mechanical advantages and disadvantages

Levers have two main functions:

- to move a load faster and further than is possible without a lever
- to move a heavier load than can be moved without a lever.

These are known as **mechanical advantages**.

Each lever system has things it can do well and not so well. The mechanical advantages and disadvantages are outlined in the table.

Lever	Advantage	Disadvantage
2nd class	👍 Provides force to lift heavy loads	👎 Small range of movement and cannot move load quickly
	Due to the load being closer to the fulcrum than the effort.	
3rd class	👍 Provides speed and wide range of movement	👎 Greater force required than the load to be moved
	Due to the effort being closer to the fulcrum than the load.	

Identifying lever systems

Each lever system can be identified by the component in the middle. If you remember the rhyme:

One,	two,	three
	=	
'F'	'L'	'E'
(fulcrum)	(load)	(effort)

Then you can remember the component in the middle and therefore name the class of lever.

Worked example

Identify the lever system operating at the knee when kicking a ball.

(1 mark)

Third class lever

You do not need to explain your answer, as it just asks you to identify the lever system.

Now try this

Explain the mechanical disadvantage of the lever system at the ball of the foot in a sprint start.　**(3 marks)**

Remember to justify your answer by linking back to the question about sprint start.

Planes and axes of movement 1

We move in planes around axes. You need to be able to identify and describe the three different body planes and axes.

Planes of movement

A plane is an imaginary line that movement direction occurs in.

You need to know the names and direction of the three different planes.

- The **sagittal plane** divides the left and right side of the body, vertically.
- The **frontal plane** divides the front and the back of the body, vertically.
- The **transverse plane** divides the top and bottom of the body, horizontally.

Axes of movement

An axis is a line about which the body/body part can turn.

You need to know the names and direction of the three different axes.

- The **sagittal axis** goes from front to back.
- The **frontal axis** goes from side to side.
- The **vertical axis** goes from top to bottom.

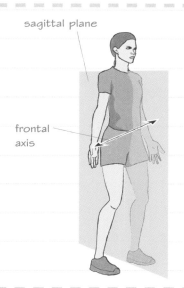
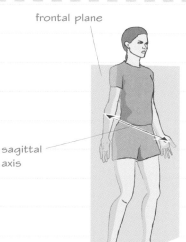
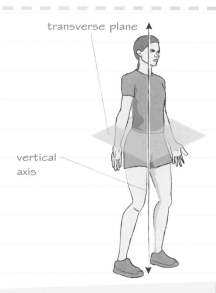

The three planes and axes of movement.

Golden rules

Remember these key facts.

- Movement in the sagittal plane can **only** be around the frontal axis, for example, when performing a front tuck somersault.
- Movement in the frontal plane can **only** be around the sagittal axis, for example, when performing a cartwheel.
- Movement in the transverse plane can **only** be around the vertical axis, for example, when performing a full twist in trampolining.

Worked example

Which is the correct description of the sagittal plane? **(1 mark)**

☒ **A** Divides the body from left to right
☐ **B** Divides the body from top to bottom
☐ **C** Divides the body from inside to out
☐ **D** Divides the body from back to front

Make sure you answer **both** parts of the question.

Now try this

Describe the direction of the frontal axis and name the plane linked with this axis. **(2 marks)**

Planes and axes of movement 2

Only certain movements can happen in each plane and around each axis. You need to be able to link the different movement possibilities to each plane and each axis, giving examples from sport.

Sagittal plane and frontal axis

The **only** movements that can occur in the sagittal plane about the frontal axis are:

- **flexion**
- **extension**.

A somersault is performed in the sagittal plane about the frontal axis.

Frontal plane and sagittal axis

The **only** movements that can occur in the frontal plane about the sagittal axis are:

- **abduction**
- **adduction**.

A cartwheel is performed in the frontal plane about the sagittal axis.

Transverse plane and vertical axis

The **only** movements that can occur in the transverse plane about the vertical axis are:

- **rotation**
- **twisting**.

A full twist is performed in the transverse plane about the vertical axis.

Worked example

Identify the movement possible in the sagittal plane.   **(1 mark)**

☐ **A** Abduction
☒ **B** Extension
☐ **C** Circumduction
☐ **D** Adduction

Remember the rules: flexion and extension are the **only** movement possibilities in the sagittal plane, so the answer must be extension.

Summary table of movement for planes and axes

Sagittal plane	Frontal plane	Transverse plane
Divides the left and right side of the body, vertically	Divides the front and back of the body, vertically	Divides the top and bottom of the body, horizontally
Flexion and extension	Abduction and adduction	Rotation
Rotation around frontal axis	Rotation around the sagittal axis	Rotation around the vertical axis
The frontal axis goes from side to side	The sagittal axis goes from front to back	The vertical axis goes from top to bottom
e.g. somersault	e.g. cartwheel	e.g. full twist in trampolining

Now try this

As part of their routine, a gymnast may perform a back somersault. Name the plane the movement occurs in **and** the axis about which the movement occurs.   **(2 marks)**

Think about the direction that the axis must be going in to allow rotation in this direction.

Fitness, health, exercise and performance

Fitness, health, exercise and performance – you need to know the difference between these terms.

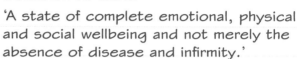

Definitions

- Questions on health, exercise and fitness often ask you to **define** one of the words.
- When asked to define, try to give a clear account of the meaning.
- If the question doesn't ask you to define but to **explain**, make sure you give a linked point as part of your explanation.

Health   Short Full

Definition to learn:

'A state of complete emotional, physical and social wellbeing and not merely the absence of disease and infirmity.'

You must remember to include all three aspects of health. If one part is missing you are not completely healthy.

Fitness   Short Full

Definition to learn:

'The ability to meet the demands of the environment.'

In other words you need to be fit enough to do what you need for your everyday life. This is different for everyone – some people only need to be fit enough to work at a desk, others need to be fit enough to complete a manual job.

Exercise

Definition to learn:

'A form of physical activity done to maintain or improve health and/or physical fitness, it is not competitive sport.'

In other words, exercise is something physical that you do in order to keep or improve the other two aspects of a healthy lifestyle – health and fitness.

Performance

Definition to learn:

'Performance means how well a task is completed.'

In other words, did they do a good job? Was the task completed well? Did they demonstrate a high level of performance? Or was the task not completed well? Did it lack fluency and accuracy or contain errors showing low performance levels?

Worked example

In order to be a good performer Jared has to be fit. Define the term fitness. **(1 mark)**

Fitness is the ability to meet the demands of the environment.

The question asks you to define, so it is best to give the exact wording given in the glossary of the specification. That way there is no doubt as to whether your answer is correct.

Now try this

Which of the following statements gives the best definition of health? **(1 mark)**

- ☐ **A** The ability to meet the demands of the environment
- ☐ **B** A state of emotional wellbeing and not merely the absence of disease and infirmity
- ☐ **C** The absence of disease
- ☐ **D** A state of complete emotional, physical and social wellbeing and not merely the absence of disease and infirmity

All options are real definitions related to your course. Make sure you select the option that offers the most accurate and most complete definition.

The relationship between health and fitness

You need to know the relationships between fitness and health, the role that exercise plays in this relationship and the impact on performance.

Factors working together

Regular **exercise** plays an important role in increasing health, fitness and performance.

- If you take part in regular exercise, you can increase your fitness.
- If your fitness improves, your performance can improve too.

For example:

> If your cardiovascular fitness improves
>
> ↓
>
> You are less likely to suffer with fatigue
>
> ↓
>
> So you can maintain your level of performance for longer.

Factors not working together `Short  Full`

> If you are not healthy enough to take part in regular exercise
>
> ↓
>
> Your fitness will deteriorate
>
> ↓
>
> Causing your performance levels to drop
>
> ↓
>
> And health benefits will not be gained

Regular exercise can also provide increased health benefits. These benefits could be physical, emotional or social.

Physical health benefits could include: `Short  Full`

- reduced chance of coronary heart disease (CHD) due to a more efficient heart and circulatory system
- reduced chance of osteoporosis due to taking part in weight-bearing exercise.

A healthy lifestyle and balanced diet will also provide increased health benefits.

regular exercise

increased fitness

increased performance

health benefits

Golden rule
Remember, exercise **must** be regular to be effective.

Worked example

Which of the following is a true statement about the relationship between exercise, health and fitness? **(1 mark)**

- ☐ **A** You need to be healthy in order to be fit
- ☐ **B** If you exercise regularly you can guarantee that you will improve health as well as fitness
- ☒ **C** It is possible to be fit but not healthy
- ☐ **D** Whatever the intensity, exercise will improve health

First, discount the obvious.
D starts with 'whatever the intensity', which isn't true as it is possible to overtrain and cause health issues.
B is false – it makes it more likely, but doesn't guarantee it.
That leaves A or C. Option C is correct – you could be fit but have a temporary illness like a cold, and therefore not be healthy.

Now try this

Explain the relationship between health and exercise. **(3 marks)**

Cardiovascular fitness

Fitness can mean different things to different sports performers. It is important to be able to break fitness down, identifying the specific components that are more relevant to some performers than others. One of these components is cardiovascular fitness, and you need to know why it is important to some performers.

Definition

Cardiovascular fitness is defined as:

'The ability to exercise the entire body for long periods of time without tiring.'

> You need both parts – 'long period of time' and 'without tiring'. Always write cardiovascular rather than the abbreviation CV, to show that you really do know the words.

The need for cardiovascular fitness

Cardiovascular fitness is required when activities:

- are mainly aerobic
- last a long time
- involve prolonged additional oxygen delivery.

It is used by performers who need to:

- maintain quality of performance over a long time, e.g. games players
- work the body for a long period of time **without tiring**, e.g. long-distance runners.

Golden rule

Short   Full

Make sure you don't confuse the term cardiovascular **fitness** with the cardiovascular **system**.

They are closely linked, as cardiovascular fitness relies on the cardiovascular system supplying oxygen, but you need to make sure you use the correct term.

Good cardiovascular fitness can be a health benefit, for example, reducing the chance of coronary heart disease (CHD).

Cardiovascular fitness is also known as **aerobic endurance**. Use whichever term you prefer – they both mean the same thing.

What, who, why and how?

When you are thinking about the components of fitness, you should ask yourself four questions:

- ☑ What is it?
- ☑ Who needs it?
- ☑ Why is it important?
- ☑ How does this affect performance?

Worked example

As a result of exercise and a healthy lifestyle, an individual may improve aspects of fitness. Which one of the following gives the best explanation of cardiovascular fitness? **(1 mark)**

- ☐ **A** The ability to exercise the muscles of the body for long periods of time without tiring
- ☐ **B** The ability to exercise the heart and lungs in the body for long periods
- ☒ **C** The ability to exercise the entire body for long periods of time without tiring
- ☐ **D** The ability to exercise the entire body for long periods of time

> At first several answers look promising, but option A mentions muscles, option B mentions heart and lungs, and although option D does state 'entire body' it does not mention 'without tiring', making option C the only one that has all relevant parts of the definition of cardiovascular fitness.

Now try this

Jo and Jus both play rugby. Cardiovascular fitness is an important component of fitness for rugby players. Briefly explain why Jo and Jus need high levels of cardiovascular fitness to perform well in their sport. **(2 marks)**

Muscular endurance

You need to know what muscular endurance is and how it is important to performance.

Definition

Muscular endurance is defined as:

'The ability to use voluntary muscles many times without getting tired.'

Golden rule

If you use a definition, make sure it is enough to answer the question. If you are asked to apply or give an example, the definition on its own will not be enough.

Avoiding confusion

Muscular endurance is:

- different from cardiovascular fitness – make sure you mention muscles!
- different from muscular strength, which is to do with force. 'Endurance' means it has to last a long time without tiring.

The need for muscular endurance

Muscular endurance is required when activities:

- are mainly aerobic
- last a long time
- require repeated use of the same muscles.

It is used by performers who need:

- prolonged additional oxygen delivery to working muscles
- to repeat muscle contractions over a long period of time **without tiring**.

Cardiovascular fitness works with muscular endurance as the heart and lungs need to supply sufficient oxygen to the working muscles so that they can contract repeatedly for a long duration.

Worked example

Define the term muscular endurance. **(1 mark)**

The ability to use voluntary muscles many times without getting tired.

Key words to include in your answer: 'muscles', 'many times', 'without tiring'.

EXAM ALERT!

It is a good idea to learn definitions for when a question states '**define**'. If a question asks you to describe or explain, you should use your own words.

Make sure you refer to Ashley's training sessions in your answer.

Now try this

Ashley has joined a rowing club and trains three times a week, rowing at least 3 kilometres every session. He is improving his muscular endurance.

Explain the term muscular endurance, using an example of how Ashley would use muscular endurance in his training sessions. **(3 marks)**

Flexibility

You need to know what flexibility is, who it is important to, and the advantages it brings to the performer if they have high levels of it.

Definition

Flexibility is defined as:

'The range of movement possible at a joint.'

Flexibility is important in **all** activities.

> **Golden rule**
>
> Ask yourself:
> - ✓ What is it?
> - ✓ Who needs it?
> - ✓ Why is it important?
> - ✓ How does this affect performance?

The importance of flexibility

Flexibility is important as it:

- increases the range of movement at the joint, allowing the performer to reach further
- helps prevent injury.

Some examples of flexibility are more obvious than others. You can see the wide range of movement at the hip and back of this gymnast.

How good flexibility benefits performance

In the examples below, note the linking words 'so' and 'because', which are used to link a fact about flexibility to its application to the activity.

Good flexibility allows the netball player to stretch further **so** she can intercept the ball.

Good flexibility prevents injury to the footballer when overstretching **because** the joint can move further before damage occurs.

Worked example

Identify how the performer on the left is using flexibility in their activity.   **(1 mark)**

The performer is using flexibility so they can reach further to get the ball.

The question asks you to 'identify', so there is no need to give a justification for your answer.

Now try this

Sue and Jenny both play basketball. Flexibility is an important component of fitness needed when playing basketball. Briefly explain why Sue and Jenny need high levels of flexibility to perform well in their sport.   **(2 marks)**

If you are asked to 'explain', don't just give a definition. You need to **give a reason why** it is important, which could be through the use of an example.

Reaction time

You need to know what reaction time is, why it is important and to be able to give examples of its use and importance to a variety of different activities.

Reaction time

Reaction time is the time it takes to respond to a **stimulus**.

Fast **reactions** are useful in events where quick decisions about movements are needed, for example:

* to get a good start
* to adapt quickly to rapid changes in play (normally game situations).

The faster the performer can react to the stimulus, the more likely it is going to help their performance.

Golden rule

When considering reaction times, always ask:

* ✓ Who? (For example, 100m sprinters.)
* ✓ What is the stimulus they respond to? (For example, starting pistol.)
* ✓ Why is it important? (For example, to get the best start.)
* ✓ How does this impact on performance? (For example, the sprinters are more likely to finish quicker.)

Identifying the stimulus

Think of different things that can be a stimulus in sporting activities:

* a ball
* a starting pistol
* a whistle
* an opponent
* an error
* a dangerous situation.

You can anticipate that something is going to happen or it may just happen suddenly, but as soon as you detect the stimulus you need to decide on a **course of action**.

In sprint activities, a fraction of a second can make the difference between winning and losing.

Other examples when a quick reaction time is needed:

* a rugby player needing to change direction quickly due to a deflected ball
* a badminton player deciding to play a different shot after their opponent has 'dummied their shot'
* a goalkeeper diving to save a sudden shot at goal
* a gymnast needing to make a sudden adjustment to an error
* a rock climber losing their footing.

Think of the benefits to each performer.

Worked example

Which of the following performers is most likely to benefit from a fast reaction time? **(1 mark)**
* ☐ **A** Rugby player performing a drop kick
* ☐ **B** Badminton player playing a smash shot
* ☐ **C** Basketball player performing a lay-up
* ☒ **D** Swimmer leaving the starting blocks

Although a good reaction time would be useful at certain points in all of these sports, the most important here is the swimmer – so they can leave the blocks quickly to win the race.

Now try this

Using this image, explain the importance of reaction time to a tennis player. **(3 marks)**

Remember to use the image to guide your answer.

Power and speed

You need to know what power and speed are and why they are important, and to be able to give examples of how they are used in a variety of different activities.

Power

Power is the ability to do strength performances quickly. In order to have power, you **must** have **strength** and **speed** together (power = strength × speed).

Golden rule

Power is all about using strength at speed. Therefore any examples you give of power must demonstrate high intensity **and** explosive movements.

This gymnast has used power to get height, so he has time to perform the move well and score points for technique.

Speed

Speed relates to the amount of time it takes to perform a particular action or cover a particular distance.

- Speed is vital in any race – a runner, cyclist or speed skater would all depend on speed.
- Speed can be vital for other movements too – a javelin thrower needs to be able to bring their arm through very fast to get the maximum distance with the javelin.

Speed is useful:

- where events are won by the quickest time
- in events where power is needed
- to gain an advantage over opponents, for example, beating them to a loose ball in football.

Who and how?

- 100-metre sprinter – to beat the opponents and get a faster time.
- Marathon runner – in a sprint finish.
- Long jumper in the run up – to jump further.
- Javelin thrower having a fast arm – to increase throwing distance.

Worked example

The picture shows a table tennis player taking part in a match. Explain, using an example, why speed is important in a table tennis match. **(3 marks)**

The player uses speed to move their arm quickly. If their arm moves quickly they can put more pace on the ball, making the shot harder for their opponent to return, and so they are more likely to win the point.

Make sure you use the word 'quickly' rather than just 'moving the arm', as the arm could be moved slowly for a soft shot. Include a justification, as the question asks you to 'explain'.

Now try this

Power is important to many different activities.
Complete the table below about power and add a different example of your own. **(5 marks)**

Who	When	Impact
Sprinter	(i)	To get an explosive start
Basketball player	(ii)	Close to hoop to score
(iii)	(iv)	(v)

Agility

You need to know what agility is and why it is important, and to be able to give examples of its use in a variety of different activities.

Agility

Agility is defined as:
'The ability to change the position of the body quickly while maintaining control of the movement.'

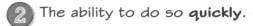

Golden rule

Note the three components of agility:

1 The ability to **change direction**.

2 The ability to do so **quickly**.

3 The ability to do so with **control**.

Describing agility

The best way to **describe** agility is:
To change direction quickly with control.

It is needed in activities where you are going in one direction and then very quickly change to a different direction, perhaps to avoid an opponent.

You need to include both 'change direction quickly' **and** 'with control' to describe agility accurately.

Ask yourself: how does being able to change direction quickly impact on performance in these sports?

Agility is very important to all games players where there is direct interaction between teams, for example, in games such as rugby, netball and football.

Agility is needed to prevent an opponent from getting free from or to dodge tackles, for example, swerving around player.

When is agility not important?

Agility is not normally important for activities where there is no interaction. Think of a 50-metre swimming race in a 50-metre pool. The swimmer has their own lane, so no one can interact with them. They only have to go one length in a straight line, so they do not need to change direction.

However, if the race is 100 metres in a 50-metre pool, then the swimmer will use agility to turn quickly to swim in the opposite direction.

Agility is also important in racket sports, such as badminton, tennis and squash.

Badminton players need to change direction quickly with control, depending on where the shuttlecock has been played.

Golden rule

Always choose an example you are sure about and use words like 'dodge' and 'swerve' when talking about agility.

Worked example

State how a basketball player will use agility in their sport. **(1 mark)**

The player will sidestep to change direction quickly with control, to avoid being tackled when dribbling down the court.

Notice how the response has been linked to the activity and uses all aspects of agility: 'change direction', 'quickly' and 'control'.

Now try this

Briefly explain how agility might be useful to a performer batting in cricket just after they have played a good shot. **(2 marks)**

Remember: What is it? Why is it important? What is the impact on the activity?

Balance and co-ordination

You need to know what balance and co-ordination are, why they are important and to be able to give examples of how they are used in a variety of different activities.

Definition

Balance is defined as:

'The ability to retain the body's centre of mass above the base of support.'

Balance can be **static** (stationary) or **dynamic** (moving). Balance is all about keeping steady to get the best result in performance.

Static balance

Static balance is when there is **no** movement and the performer needs to hold the position still.

Static balance is important to the gymnast so she does not fall or wobble and lose points for the quality of her movement.

Dynamic balance

Dynamic balance is balance while moving in an activity.

Dynamic balance is important to the hammer thrower so he maintains balance while turning and does not step out of the area, causing a foul throw.

Both types of balance are important to the performers.

Co-ordination

Co-ordination is defined as:

'The ability to use two or more body parts together.'

The movement needs to be controlled so the end result is:

- efficient
- smooth
- effective.

All physical activities require good co-ordination to be successful.

Describing co-ordination

When describing co-ordination you **must**:

- mention that it involves **two** or more body parts
- mention that they are used **at the same time** or **together**.

For example, a tennis player will need to use their hand and eyes together to ensure successful contact is made between the ball and the racket in order to play an effective shot.

Worked example

Briefly explain how a football player uses co-ordination to take a shot at goal. **(2 marks)**

The player will use foot–eye co-ordination so that the foot accurately makes contact with the ball. This will enable them to execute the technique correctly, making good contact and increasing the accuracy of their shot at the goal.

When answering questions about co-ordination you need to be very clear about:

- Which two body parts are co-ordinating?
- Why is this good?
- What will the impact be on performance?

Now try this

Describe the difference between how co-ordination is used by a golfer taking a putt and a swimmer during a 100-metre butterfly race.

(4 marks)

Body composition and strength

You need to know what body composition and strength are and why they are important, and you need to be able to give examples of how each is used in a variety of different activities.

Body composition

Body composition is defined as:
'The relative ratio of fat mass to fat-free mass in the body.'

All performers will have different amounts of fat compared to fat-free mass depending on the nature of the activity.

If a performer has the optimum ratio (the best amount of each) for their activity, this should help their performance.

Consider these examples.

- If a long-distance runner has too much muscle, the additional weight of the muscle will make it harder to cover the distance they need to run, thus slowing their times. If they have too much fat, although not as heavy as muscle, this will still slow them down as it is excess weight.

- If a rugby prop doesn't have enough muscle and body fat, it would be easier for their opponents to push them off the ball.

- A sprinter will need a low ratio of body fat to muscle to maximise their power.

Strength

Strength is defined as:
'The amount of force a muscle can exert against resistance.'

Who needs it?	Why is it important?
Weightlifter	To lift heavy weights
Gymnast	To support own body weight
Games player	To not get pushed off the ball

Golden rule

Be careful not to confuse strength with muscular endurance. For strength, the emphasis is on exerting as great a force as possible – so by definition it could not be done many times, unlike muscular endurance.

Be careful not to confuse strength with power. Strength can be used on its own, unlike power, which is a combination of strength and speed.

Worked example

Complete the table below by giving an example of how strength would be used by each performer.   **(3 marks)**

Performer	How strength is used in their activity
Sprinter	The sprinter would use strength to apply a greater force against the ground or starting block to decrease the time taken to run the race.
Rugby player	A rugby player would use strength to stop himself being barged off the ball; this would allow him to maintain possession.
Weightlifter	A weightlifter would use strength to support a heavy weight above his head at the end of the lift for a short period of time.

Use the phrase 'short period of time' to show that you are talking about strength and **not** muscular endurance. This is an example of the **impact** of strength on performance.

Now try this

State how body composition and strength are important to the gymnast in the picture.   **(2 marks)**

PARQ and fitness tests

You need to be able to assess if you or someone else is ready to take part in training and recommend training levels based on a PARQ. You also need to know the advantages of fitness testing.

PARQ

This is the **Physical Activity Readiness Questionnaire**.

Taking part in physical activity has many health benefits, but for some people, taking part might not be appropriate as it could make a current health condition worse.

A PARQ is designed to identify any potential health problems that mean physical exercise would not be recommended.

Typical PARQ questions

A PARQ would include questions about:

- personal physical details (for example, weight)
- family health history (for example, any incidence of coronary heart disease)
- known health problems (for example, high blood pressure)
- lifestyle (for example, smoking).

Use of PARQ questions

The information gathered can be used to make recommendations for training.

Fitness tests

To assess fitness levels in order to develop an appropriate exercise programme, you need to:

- know the fitness requirements for a selection of different activities
- know the tests that measure each of the components of fitness
- be able to interpret the results of the tests
- make recommendations based on the results.

Use of fitness tests

Fitness tests should **never** be part of a training session.

How and why?

Fitness tests are used:

- at the start of an exercise programme
- during a programme to monitor how the training is going
- at the end of the programme to see if it has worked.

Reasons for fitness testing include:

- establishing your current level of fitness
- identifying strengths and weaknesses in fitness
- using this information to plan a relevant training programme
- helping you set SMART targets
- checking for improvements in fitness since the last test.

Worked example

The student in the picture is completing a questionnaire before undertaking physical activity for the first time at his new club.

(2 marks)

(a) Name the type of questionnaire the student is most likely to be completing?

PARQ

(b) Give an example of a 'typical' question that might be asked on the questionnaire.

Do you smoke? If yes, how many cigarettes do you smoke a day?

There is no need to write 'physical activity readiness questionnaire' in full when answering this type of question.

Now try this

Explain why family health history is asked for in a PARQ.

(2 marks)

Cardiovascular fitness tests

You need to be able to select the appropriate fitness test for specific components of fitness and give a rationale for your selection. You also need to be able to describe the **test protocols** and interpret test results.

Cooper 12-minute run test

Working with a partner, one runs, one counts the number of laps.

- Run (or run/walk) for 12 minutes.
- Calculate the distance run based on the length of the track, for example, 400 metres.
- Compare your result to a rating chart.

Cooper 12-minute swim test

Working with a partner, one swims, one counts the number of lengths.

- Swim for 12 minutes.
- Calculate the distance swum based on the length of the pool.
- Compare your result to a rating chart.

Harvard step test

- Step up and down on to a bench (33 cm for women or 40 cm for men).
- Continue for 5 minutes (1 step every 2 seconds, usually to the beat of a metronome).
- When finished, take your heart rate (HR) for 30 seconds at 1 minute, 2 minutes and 3 minutes after the test. Add the three HRs together.
- Complete the following calculation: 100 × 300 (seconds) divided by the sum of the three HRs.
- Compare your result to a rating chart.

Using charts

These tests could be used by performers take part in endurance activities (those that last a long time), such as games players, long-distance runners and swimmers.

The chart below is a rating chart showing **normative data**.

It is not unusual for different charts for the same test to have slightly different figures. To make sure your results are consistent, always use the same chart each time you test.

Group	Excellent	Good	Average	Slow
Boys 13–14	+2700	2400–2699	2200–2399	2100–2199
Girls 13–14	+2000	1900–1999	1600–1899	1500–1599
Boys 15–16	+2800	2500–2799	2300–2499	2200–2299
Girls 15–16	+2100	2000–2099	1700–1999	1600–1699
Boys 17–20	+3000	2700–2999	2500–2699	2300–2499
Girls 17–20	+2300	2100–2299	1800–2099	1700–1799

Cooper 12-minute run test rating

Harvard step test rating

	Excellent	Above average	Average	Below average	Poor
Male	>90	80–90	65–79	55–64	<55
Female	>86	76–86	61–75	50–60	<50

Key terms

- **Normative data** – the name given to the rating charts that you use to determine your test results.
- **Test protocol** – how the test is carried out.

Worked example

Before starting their training programme, Zoe and Niamh completed the Cooper 12-minute swim test. Zoe swam 350 metres and Niamh swam 620 metres.

Use the ratings chart to determine which performer will need to train more on their cardiovascular fitness. **(1 mark)**

Excellent	>640 m
Good	549–639 m
Fair	457–548 m
Poor	366–456 m
Very poor	<366 m

Zoe will need to train more on her cardiovascular fitness, as her result was very poor.

Now try this

Name the test that would be most suitable in the following situation: a large group with access to a field, who want to test their cardiovascular endurance. **(1 mark)**

Strength and flexibility tests

When selecting appropriate tests before training for a specific sport, think about the components of fitness required and then select the most appropriate tests for those areas of fitness.

Grip dynamometer

Test of:

- strength (hand and forearm).

Used for:

- activities where strength in the hand is important, for example, rock climbing.

Golden rule

Do not say that fitness tests are used 'to **improve**' any named component of fitness. This is a common mistake. **They are not!** Fitness tests 'test'. 'Training' is used to improve.

Test protocol:

- Use a grip dynamometer.
- Adjust the grip to fit your hand.
- Keep your arm beside and at a right angle to body.
- Squeeze the handle as hard as you can.
- Compare your result to a rating chart.

Sit and reach test

Test of:

- flexibility (lower back and hamstrings).

Test used by:

- gymnasts
- hurdlers.

Test protocol:

- Use a sit and reach box.
- Sit with legs straight and soles of feet flat against box.
- Palms face down, one hand on top of the other on box top, stretch and reach as far as possible.
- Record distance reached.
- Compare your result to a rating chart.

Worked example

Discuss the value of the grip dynamometer test for measuring strength relevant to sprinting. **(9 marks)**

The grip dynamometer test is a test of strength so has some relevance, but it is a measure of grip strength, not the strength required by sprinters. Therefore it would be better to find a test that related to leg strength for the sprinters.

If a question starts with the word 'Discuss', this normally means that you need to think of good points and bad points relating to the topic and then come to a conclusion at the end. This answer identifies a good point (tests strength), ✓ a bad point (leg strength more relevant to sprinters) ✓ and concludes (look for a test for leg strength) ✓. This is the first paragraph of an extended answer question, demonstrating knowledge, application and evaluation.

Now try this

Liam is 14 years old. He has returned to gymnastics after injury. He completed the sit and reach test and scored 23 cm. Explain how Liam's coach would use the information from this fitness test. **(3 marks)**

Use of data

Rating	Age (years)				
	12	13	14	15	16
Good	29	30	33	34	36
Average	26	26	28	30	30
Below average	20	21	23	24	25

Agility and speed tests

Agility tests are used by performers who need to change direction quickly, while speed tests are used by performers who need to run fast for short periods of time.

Illinois agility run

Test of: **agility**.

Test used by:

- basketball players
- rugby players.

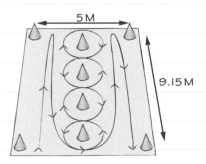

5 M

9.15 M

Test protocol:

- Set up the course as shown in the picture.
- Lie face down on the floor by the first cone.
- On 'GO', run round the course as fast as possible.
- Record the time taken.
- Compare your result to a rating chart.

30-metre sprint

Test of: **speed**.

Test used by:

- 100-metre sprinters
- rugby players.

Test protocol:

- Measure and mark out 30 metres in a straight line.
- Place one cone at the start and one at the end.
- On 'GO', run as fast as you can.
- Record the time taken.
- Compare your result to a rating chart.

Worked example

Name the fitness test being described below.

Start from a stationary position and when told to 'go', run as fast as possible in a straight line.

(1 mark)

30-metre sprint

Most tests will start from a stationary position, so this part of the description doesn't really help. However, the description then says 'run as fast as possible'. That implies speed, so it could be the Illinois agility run test or the 30-metre sprint. The final part of the description says 'in a straight line' so must be referring to the 30-metre sprint, as the Illinois agility run test requires changes in direction.

Now try this

Imran plays for the school football team. At the start of the season the team undergoes a series of fitness tests. In the table below:

- tick the most relevant fitness test for a football player (not goalkeeper)
- explain why this fitness test is most relevant to Imran.   **(3 marks)**

Fitness tests	Tick (✓)	Explanation: why this fitness test is the most relevant to Imran.
Illinois agility run test		
Grip dynamometer		
Sit and reach test		

Power and muscular endurance tests

You need to know the difference between these fitness tests: power tests are short explosive tests whereas muscular endurance tests use repeated muscle contractions for 1 minute.

Vertical jump test

Test of: **power (legs)**.

Test used by:

- sprinters
- rugby players.

Test protocol:

- Stand side on to a wall, feet flat on the floor.
- Mark the highest point where the tips of your fingers can reach with the arm closest to the wall.
- Holding a piece of chalk in the hand closest to the wall, jump as high as you can (upwards).
- Mark the wall at the top of the jump.
- Measure the difference between the first and second chalk marks.
- Compare your result to a rating chart.

One-minute press-up test

Test of: **muscular endurance**.

Test protocol:

- Working with a partner, one times the test and keeps count, one completes the test.
- Lie flat on a mat (face down), hands by shoulders.
- Push up, extending arms until straight.
- Lower until elbows at 90°.
- Push up again.
- Complete as many as you can in one minute.
- Compare your result to a rating chart.

One-minute press-up test.

One-minute sit-up test

Test of: **muscular endurance**.

Test protocol:

- Working with a partner, one times the test and keeps count, one completes the test.
- Lie on a mat, knees bent, feet on floor.
- Place arms across chest, hands on opposite shoulders.
- Sit up until back is at 90° then return to start position
- Complete as many as you can in one minute.
- Compare your result to a rating chart.

One-minute sit-up test.

Worked example

Explain whether you would use the one-minute sit-up test or vertical jump test with a high jump performer.

(4 marks)

As the question asks for an explanation you need to justify your answer.

The sit-up test is a test of muscular endurance, the vertical jump test is a test of power. A high jumper does not need muscular endurance as their event is explosive, but they do need power to clear the bar, therefore they should use the vertical jump test.

Now try this

State why the one-minute press-up test would be relevant to test the fitness of a rower.

(2 marks)

Interpreting fitness test results

You need to be able to collect and interpret data from fitness tests and analyse and evaluate the results against normative data tables.

Collecting data

When collecting results from a series of fitness tests you will need to produce a **data collection sheet**. This should include:

- the date
- the name of the test
- your result
- the outcome based on your comparison to the relevant rating chart.

This will help you see if your training programme has been successful.

Key terms

- **Raw data** – the score from your fitness test.
- **Interpret** – using the data tables to provide a rating of your fitness.
- **Analyse** – break down the information to determine where your strengths/weaknesses are based on the test results.
- **Evaluate** – make a judgement based on looking at the data about the impact of training.

Worked example

The table below shows normative data for the Cooper 12-minute run for females.

Watch out for these symbols in the data tables:
< = less than
> = greater than

Age	Excellent	Above average	Average	Below average	Poor
13–14	>2000 m	1900–2000 m	1600–1899 m	1500–1599 m	<1500 m
15–16	>2100 m	2000–2100 m	1700–1999 m	1600–1699 m	<1600 m
17–19	>2300 m	2100–2300 m	1800–2099 m	1700–1799 m	<1700 m

Use of data

Eve is 19 and her younger sister Nell is 14. They both ran 2100 metres in the Cooper 12-minute run. Use the table above to interpret the scores and evaluate their results. **(4 marks)**

Nell's score was greater than 2000 metres, meaning her rating was excellent for a 14-year-old. Eve's score places her above average for a 19-year-old. As both ratings are above average they may wish to focus their training on another area where they need to make greater improvements.

Find the score on the chart to determine the rating and then evaluate the information. If you score excellent or above average you might not wish to specifically train on this component of fitness but work on one where you scored average or below. Average is OK but if you want to improve performance you should be aiming for higher.

Now try this

State why it is important to analyse and evaluate fitness test results. **(2 marks)**

Progressive overload

To improve your fitness you need to train. When planning a training programme you need to use the principles of training. You need to be able to describe, explain and apply these principles.

Principles of training

For training to be successful it is important that you do not train too little or too much. It is also important that the training is right for each person, and will help them to improve. In order to make sure this happens you need to apply the principles of training.

> **Golden rule**
>
> Do not confuse **principles** of training with **methods** of training.
>
> - Principles are the things you need to consider when planning your training programme.
> - Methods are the ways you complete your training.

> **F I R S T O P**
>
> The principles you need to take into account when planning training are:
>
> F = FITT
> I = Individual needs
> R = Reversibility
> S = Specificity
> T = Thresholds of training
> O = Overtraining
> P = Progressive overload.
> F I R S T O P – some of these principles should be **applied** and some should be **avoided**; however, you need to consider them all.

Progressive overload

Progressive overload must show an increase in training over time and it must be gradual so that no injuries occur.

Description:

- Progressive overload means gradually increasing the amount of work in training so that fitness gains occur, but without the potential for injury.

Explanation:

- You need to gradually increase intensity in training so that the body continues to increase fitness.

Application:

- Week 1 = do 5 sit ups.
- Week 2 = do 10 sit ups.

 Don't confuse the word 'overload' with 'overuse'. You should overload but not overuse, which is forcing yourself beyond your capabilities.

Worked example

Briefly explain the principle of progressive overload, and state how it can improve fitness. **(2 marks)**

Progressive overload means gradually increasing the work you do. For example, if you lift heavier weights, you will get stronger, therefore fitter because the body adapts to the new workload.

There needs to be a definition and an example, a link between the principle and why fitness increases. It would not be enough to just say you get stronger.

Now try this

Jamie wanted to improve his cardiovascular fitness by developing a Personal Exercise Programme (PEP) based on continuous training.

Explain how Jamie could use progressive overload to improve his cardiovascular fitness. **(3 marks)**

Specificity

You need to know how to apply the principle of specificity to your personal exercise programme (PEP).

Specificity

Description:

- Specificity means matching training to the particular requirements of an activity.

Explanation:

- You must make sure that your training is appropriate for your sport. This is so that you are training the right muscles and body systems, rather than other areas of fitness that will have little impact on your performance.

Application:

- For specificity, a rower could plan their training around using a rowing machine.

Golden rule

Don't confuse specificity with individual needs – specificity is about the requirements of the activity, not the person!

Training

Activity

Using a treadmill instead of a rowing machine may train some of the same things but would not be the best match.

Show your understanding

If you are asked to define or explain specificity, don't just use the word 'specific' in your answer. You need to demonstrate your understanding of the **principle** of specificity.

Worked example

Which of the following statements does not conform to the principle of specificity? **(1 mark)**

- ☐ **A** A 100 m runner practising their sprint starts
- ☐ **B** A games player taking part in a fartlek training session
- ☐ **C** A tennis player practising their first serves
- ☒ **D** A 50 m freestyle swimmer working on their speed at the track

EXAM ALERT!

Be careful not to confuse individual differences with specificity. Remember, specificity relates to the needs of the activity.

The swimmer should be training in the pool rather than on the track.

Now try this

Three items of fitness training equipment are shown here.

Explain which of the items of equipment shown is most likely to be used by a sprint cyclist. **(3 marks)**

Individual needs and overtraining

There are two principles of training covered on this page – one you need to use in your PEP, and one you need to plan to avoid!

Individual needs

Description:

- This means matching the training to the requirements of the individual person.

Explanation:

- It is very important to make sure the training is appropriate for the person, as everyone is different. For example, although two people might play the same position in football, if one has higher levels of fitness, they will not benefit from following a fitness programme designed for the less fit player.

Application:

- Remmy is 13 and her brother is 16. They both play football. Remmy trains twice a week for 30 minutes; however, her brother trains every other day for 60 minutes.

Golden rule

Unlike specificity, individual needs are about the person and not the activity.

Note how the training varies because of the differences between the two individuals. The differences in age and sex are likely to mean that Remmy's brother will be physically able to withstand a higher intensity of training, therefore he trains more than his younger sister.

Overtraining Short Full

This means doing too much training, which can lead to injury and prevent improvement.

Overtraining may be due to many reasons, such as:

- inadequate rest between sessions, so there is no time to recover
- making sessions too long
- using a workload that is too high.

To prevent overtraining, sessions should be planned applying the principles of training, so that there are rest days and the workload/time is increased gradually.

Without appropriate recovery, adaptations will not happen.

If injury occurs due to overtraining, your training programme may be interrupted and **reversibility** could take place (see page 50).

 Worked example

Glen is a good gymnast. He is trying to improve by following a training programme based on improving flexibility and speed. Glen's coach has given him a different training programme to the one his friend is following, who is also a gymnast. Why might the coach do this? **(1 mark)**

Following the principle of individual needs, the coach is making sure the training matches the individual's needs not just the activity.

 Now try this

Explain why you should consider the principle of overtraining when planning your training programme. **(3 marks)**

 Remember to justify your answer as the question asks you to **explain**.

FITT and reversibility

You need to be able to explain the components of the FITT principle: Frequency, Intensity, Time and Type. You also need to be able to explain the term 'reversibility', why it might occur and what its impact on performance might be.

FITT: Frequency

This is about **how often** you train. It should be gradually increased, for example:

Once a fortnight to start with → Once a week → Twice a week

Training more often can lead to improved performance.

FITT: Intensity

This is about **how hard** you train. It should be gradually increased, for example:

• 1 set of 5 repetitions of a 5 kg weight.
• 2 sets of 5 repetitions of a 5 kg weight.
• 2 sets of 5 repetitions of a 10 kg weight.

Training harder can lead to improved performance.

FITT: Time

This is about how long you train. It should be gradually increased, for example:

Session 1 = 20 minutes → Session 2 = 25 minutes → Session 3 = 30 minutes

Training for longer can lead to improved performance.

FITT: Type

This relates to specificity. The closer the match between the type of training and the activity, the better the improvement in performance.

Worked example

As part of her practical exam, Jackie was asked how she applied the FITT principle in her PEP. Describe how Jackie could apply one of the components of the FITT principle. **(1 mark)**

Jackie could increase the frequency of her training. She may have started training once a week and increased it to twice a week in the second week of her PEP.

Overlap with other principles

The FITT components should be taken into account when applying progressive overload, but remember the principle of overtraining and its impact.

Reversibility

This means that any improvement or change that takes place as a consequence of training will be reversed when you stop training.

Just as fitness can be increased through training, the benefits will be lost if training stops due to injury or a holiday.

Now try this

The FITT principle of training is made up of four parts. Which of the following statements covers all four parts? **(1 mark)**

☐ **A** How hard and often you work, making sure you do not do too much, whilst avoiding boredom

☐ **B** How long, hard and often you work, whilst maintaining safety

☐ **C** How hard and often you work, making sure that your training fits the requirements of the activity, and that you do not do too much

☐ **D** How long, hard and often you work, making sure that your training fits the requirements of the activity

Thresholds of training

When planning training programmes you need to be able to set the relevant thresholds of training for your requirements using a simplified version of the Karvonen formula.

Training within your target zone

To maximise the chance of fitness adaptations taking place, you should train within your target zone.

The area of the target zone you aim to work within depends upon the intensity of your activity or the aim of your training programme.

If your activity has lots of high intensity work, you should aim to work nearer the upper threshold of your target zone.

Your anaerobic training zone is:

• 80 to 90% of your max heart rate (MHR).

If your activity is mainly low intensity or you wish to use fat as an energy source, you should aim to work nearer the lower threshold of your target zone.

Your aerobic training zone is:

• 60 to 80% of your MHR.

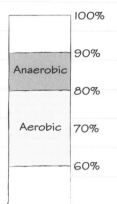

Maths skills **The Karvonen formula**

This is the simplified version of the Karvonen formula that you need to know. Use it to estimate your target zones:

Your starting number is always 220.

220 minus your age (or any age you are given) gives you a MHR.

Then calculate 80% and 60% of your MHR.

You will have two HR figures: 80% is the upper threshold of your aerobic training and 60% is the lower threshold of your aerobic training zone.

Examples of calculating aerobic training zones:

• Bobbie is 16 years old

$$220 - 16 = 204 \quad \text{(MHR)}$$
$$80 \times 204 \div 100 = 163 \quad \text{(80%)}$$
$$60 \times 204 \div 100 = 122 \quad \text{(60%)}$$

You can round figures up and down, so Bobbie's training zone is between 160 and 120 beats per minute (bpm).

• Lauren is 35 years old

$$220 - 35 = 185 \quad \text{(MHR)}$$
$$80 \times 185 \div 100 = 148 \quad \text{(80%)}$$
$$60 \times 185 \div 100 = 111 \quad \text{(60%)}$$

Her training zone is between 150 and 110 bpm.

Worked example

If the correct target zone for an endurance athlete is 120–160 bpm, how old is the athlete?   **(1 mark)**

☐ A 15   ☒ B 20   ☐ C 25   ☐ D 40

You would need to use the target heart rate calculation to answer this question:
220 − age = maximum HR.
220 − 20 = 200
60% of 200 is 120 bpm
80% of 200 is 160 bpm

Now try this

State which of the lines on the graph (A, B, C or D) would indicate that Sulliman (aged 16) was working within his aerobic target zone whilst training?   **(1 mark)**

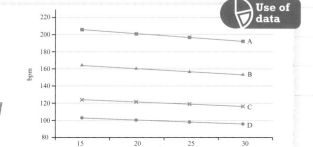

Use the information in the graph to guide you, and remember that there should be an upper and a lower limit to a target zone.

Continuous training

You need to know six methods of training and the relevance of each to different activities.

Methods of training

Methods of training are used to improve fitness and performance levels. You need to be able to describe the methods of training and explain how they can improve fitness.

You should be able to select the most appropriate method based on:

- your level of fitness
- the requirements of the sport
- the facilities available.

Aerobic or anaerobic

You need to know which methods of training should be used to develop fitness for aerobic activities, and which for anaerobic activities.

- Interval training is used more for anaerobic activities.
- Continuous training is aerobic and is therefore used more for aerobic endurance-based activities.

Aerobic activities are **sub-maximal**. This means you do not work flat out and so can continue to work for long periods of time.

Continuous training: characteristics

In continuous training, each training session:

- should be for 20 minutes or longer
- must not involve any breaks during the session.

For example: run at a steady pace around a 400-metre track for 30 minutes (without stopping).

Activities associated with continuous training

- ☑ Long-distance running.
- ☑ Long-distance cycling.
- ☑ Long-distance swimming.

Continuous training: benefits   Short Full

Components of fitness that would improve with continuous training include:

- cardiovascular fitness
- muscular endurance.

Regular continuous training can reduce the chance of coronary heart disease and related illnesses.

Golden rule

All methods of training, if done on a regular basis over a period of time, will bring about fitness adaptations, such as:

- lower resting heart rate
- decreased recovery time.

 Worked example

What type of activity would an athlete probably be involved in if they only used continuous training to improve their fitness?   **(1 mark)**

They are likely to be involved in an endurance event, for example, marathon running.

Remember that 'athlete' is a term that can be used to mean any sports performer, not just those participating in 'athletics'.

 Now try this

Briefly explain why a long-distance runner would use continuous training as their main training method.

(2 marks)

Fartlek training

Fartlek training is a form of **continuous training**. Its key characteristics are variations in pace and terrain covered.

Key benefits

Jogging on the road

Sprinting on the road

Grassy hill

Changes of pace allow for recovery so performer can work maximally.

Fartlek training improves cardiovascular fitness and muscular endurance and reduces the chance of coronary heart disease.

Fartlek training is continuous, but the changes in pace within the sessions mean that performers work both aerobically (jogging) and anaerobically (sprinting, running uphill) within the exercise session.

Activities associated with fartlek training

(Netball)   (Hockey)   (Rugby)   (Basketball)

This is due to the similarity between the training method and the game situation where there is sprinting and recovery, for example, making a fast break in hockey and then jogging back into position.

Worked example

Some training activities can be **adapted** to suit different performance activities. How might a cross-country runner and a footballer adapt fartlek training to suit their own activity?

(2 marks)

A cross-country runner would focus on changing terrains, for example, up and down hills.

A footballer would focus on variation in pace to match game requirements.

EXAM ALERT!

Make sure you read the questions carefully – you need to say how the training session is adapted, not just explain the training method.

Now try this

If you are a games player, why should you involve jogging and sprinting in a fartlek session?   **(2 marks)**

Think about what a games player does during the game.

53

Circuit training

Circuit training involves a chain of different activities that can be selected to suit individual or activity requirements.

Can be used to develop all of the components of fitness depending on the nature of the stations included, e.g.
- sit-ups for muscular endurance
- shuttle runs for speed
- dodging through cones for agility
- balancing ball for balance.

There are a number of stations (usually between 6 and 12).

The stations are organised in a circuit, so that you can progress from one station to the next.

The stations can be fitness- or skill-based.

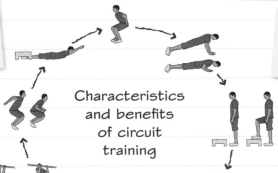

Characteristics and benefits of circuit training

Can be organised so that it is continuous, usually done with 30–60 second breaks while leaving one station and getting in position at the next – **interval training**.

The variety of stations allows recovery of muscle groups (so anaerobic work is possible).

Aerobic circuit training will have the health benefits associated with this type of activity, for example, weight loss if overweight through burning additional calories.

The intensity can be measured by:
- the **time** at each station
- the **number of repetitions** at each station
- the **number of circuits** completed.

Depending on the intensity of the activity, circuit training can be aerobic (low intensity) or anaerobic (high intensity).

Worked example

George is 15 years old. He has designed a circuit to help improve his performance in basketball and badminton.

Four of the circuit stations are listed below:

Station 1 – running in and out of cones
Station 2 – lay-up shots using a basketball and basketball ring
Station 3 – bowling at a target
Station 4 – badminton serves.

Explain why one of these stations is not appropriate for George's circuit.   **(2 marks)**

Station 3, bowling at a target, does not relate to either of his sports.

Now try this

State three characteristics of circuit training.   **(3 marks)**

Remember, **do not** use fitness tests as circuit stations.

Interval training

You need to know what interval training is and when it would be an appropriate method of training to use.

Characteristics

This type of training has periods of intense activity, with breaks within the session to allow recovery.

A typical session is usually made up of:

- sets of high intensity work (e.g. sprint)
- followed by rest or low intensity work (active rest)
- followed by high intensity work (e.g. sprint)
- followed by rest or low intensity work (active rest).

Aerobic and anaerobic

Aerobic – 'with oxygen' (low intensity, longer duration activities).

Anaerobic – 'without oxygen' (short lived, explosive activities).

Benefits

- Aerobic interval training will have the health benefits associated with this type of activity, for example, weight loss (if overweight) due to burning calories.
- It is a very flexible training method that can be used to improve health and fitness in a range of ways.
- Although normally associated with powerful and explosive activities, it can be adapted to work on cardiovascular fitness by altering the lengths of the rest periods.

If you are asked to name a method of training to improve cardiovascular fitness, only use interval training if you can **clearly** justify your answer by explaining how it can be adapted.

Forms of interval training

These include:

- training on a track
- circuit training
- weight training.

Although interval training can be designed for both aerobic and anaerobic activity, it is usually associated with shorter anaerobic events such as sprinting and is a major form of training for swimmers.

Interval training methods can be designed so that most components of fitness can be improved through an interval training programme. Strength could be improved if breaks are programmed in to a weight training session, for example:

- 10 reps arms, rest arms
- 10 reps legs, rest legs
- 10 reps arms, rest arms.

Worked example

Explain how you could tell by looking at a performer's interval training session plan if they were an endurance or power athlete. **(2 marks)**

Fewer rest intervals for an endurance athlete than for a power athlete and less intense workload during period of work for an endurance athlete compared to a power athlete.

Make sure you make it clear which type of performer you are talking about.

Now try this

Interval training is a method of training that can be used by a variety of performers.

Describe **three** characteristics of interval training. **(3 marks)**

'Characteristics' means things that are specific to that method of training.

Plyometric training

You need to be able to decide when plyometric training would be an appropriate method to use.

Characteristics of plyometric training

- Jumping/bounding (often over obstacles).
- High intensity.
- Short duration.
- Breaks between sets.
- Speed not endurance.
- Maximal.

Benefits of plyometric training

- Used to develop power by quickly lengthening and then quickly shortening muscles.
- Used to train for activities where there are fast explosive movements, such as:
  - volleyball
  - basketball
  - hurdles.

There are different types of plyometrics for different activities. The type of plyometrics you use will depend on:

- what you want to train for
- the resources available
- your level of fitness.

Plyometrics can be used to develop power in the upper or lower body. For example:

- explosive press-ups or catching and throwing a medicine ball will help develop the upper body
- bounding and jumping will develop the lower body.

Plyometrics can be completed by jumping onto boxes, jumping high and fast. This could be used when training for basketball, where the performer needs to jump high when taking a shot.

Worked example

Describe **two** ways that the intensity of plyometric training could be increased to provide progressive overload to a training session.

(2 marks)

The training session can be adjusted to make it gradually harder, for example, by gradually increasing the height of the box and also increasing the number of boxes.

Make sure you include **two** answers. If you don't know the answer, think about the activity: what could you change to make it harder?

Now try this

Explain why plyometric training would be a suitable method of training for a volleyball player.

(3 marks)

Think of the activity (volleyball): think of the component of fitness that plyometric training will improve, and how a volleyball player uses this component of fitness in their sport.

Weight/resistance training

You need to know how weight training can be carried out to develop different components of fitness.

Characteristics of weight training

The key characteristics are:

- a form of **interval training** using weights
- involves 'reps and sets' – the weights are lifted a number of times (reps), followed by a break before starting another set
- weight provides a resistance or load for the muscles to work against.

Golden rule

When referring to this method of training, make sure to always state **weight training** or **resistance training** and not weights or weightlifting.

Using weight training

Weight training can be completed by using machines or free weights.

The muscles you wish to train can be targeted by doing specific exercises, for example, biceps curls work on the biceps!

Benefits

Weight training can be used to develop fitness for many activities, the most obvious being those requiring **power** and **strength**.

For example:

- weight lifting
- rugby
- shot put.

It can also be used for activities requiring **muscular endurance**, for example, tennis.

The components of fitness developed due to weight training depend on the design of your training session.

For example:

- to develop **power** and **strength** use high weight × low number of reps
- to develop **muscular endurance** use low weight × high number of reps.

Worked example

Ria has taken up discus and wants to know what training method to use to help improve her performance. Explain which training method she should use. **(2 marks)**

Weight training – as this will help her increase her strength so she can throw the discus further.

Make sure you answer **both** parts of the question. If you can justify your choice, you know you must have made a good decision.

Now try this

Endurance and power athletes will often use weight training as part of their training programme. Describe how weight training can be used to develop muscular strength or muscular endurance. **(2 marks)**

Fitness classes

You need to know that, in addition to methods of training, there are fitness classes that you can attend to improve specific components of fitness for physical activity and sport. Classes can be more fun than training on your own, as there is an instructor to help provide motivation.

Aerobics

Develops: cardiovascular endurance.

- There are many different types of aerobics class.
- All involve continuous activity for between 30 and 60 minutes.

'Step aerobics' class.

Body pump

Develops: muscular endurance or strength.

- Moderate to high intensity.
- Uses barbells.
- Lots of repetitions.
- Targets all areas of the body.

Body pump uses barbells to develop muscular endurance or strength.

Pilates

Develops: flexibility, balance and strength.

- Exercises done on a mat.
- Uses resistance.
- Focus is on core muscles.

Pilates instructor providing resistance.

Yoga

Develops: flexibility, balance and strength.

- Exercises done on a mat.
- Also includes a relaxation phase.

Yoga develops flexibility, balance and strength.

Spinning

Develops: cardiovascular endurance and muscular endurance.

- Continuous cycling to music with an instructor to motivate.
- Pace changes throughout.

Spinning class.

Worked example

State one similarity and one difference between Pilates and yoga. **(2 marks)**

Pilates and yoga can both improve flexibility. However, yoga also involves meditation/relaxation techniques.

Now try this

Explain why some rugby teams use aerobics classes as part of their training. **(3 marks)**

 Think about the component of fitness being developed in an aerobics class and how this component of fitness might benefit rugby players.

Training methods: pros and cons

You need to know what is good and what is not so good about the different methods of training. Think about things you like and don't like when doing each method.

Continuous training
👍 No equipment or facilities needed.
👍 Can do on your own or with others.
👍 Health benefits (e.g. reduced chance of CHD).
👎 Can be boring, so motivation can be lost.
👎 Doesn't change pace, so not so good for games players.
👎 Can cause impact injuries.

Fartlek training
👍 No equipment or facilities needed.
👍 Can do on your own or with others.
👍 Change of pace/terrain can add interest.
👎 Safe route not always easy to find.
👎 Higher intensity parts can be avoided.

Circuit training
👍 Variety of stations generates interest.
👍 Does not have to involve equipment.
👍 Can work on skill and fitness.
👍 Can be aerobic or anaerobic by changing the time at stations/rest.
👍 Easily adapted for each person.
👎 If equipment is required, can be costly.
👎 Can take time to set up and put away.
👎 Limited time at stations to work on skills.
👎 Difficult to work on all skills.

Interval training
👍 No equipment needed.
👍 Can be adapted for anaerobic or aerobic activity.
👎 Can be repetitive and therefore boring.
👎 Need to plan and keep track of sets.

Plyometric training
👍 Can be completed with no equipment.
👎 Can cause injury due to its high intensity if not carried out correctly.

Weight/resistance training
👍 Easily adapted for muscular endurance or strength.
👍 Can target specific areas of the body.
👎 Equipment can be expensive.
👎 Need to complete technique correctly to avoid injury.
👎 Free weights need to have a spotter.

 Worked example

Give a disadvantage of fartlek training for a sprinter. **(2 marks)**

Although fartlek includes sprints, a sprinter would not need to work on their cardiovascular fitness and would therefore not be focusing on their anaerobic system.

 Does the method match the event?

 Now try this

One disadvantage of continuous training is that it can get boring. Explain why this is a disadvantage. **(3 marks)**

 This is an 'explain' question, so refer to the impact on the performer.

The effects and benefits of exercise to the skeletal system

Over time, if done correctly, regular training and exercise will benefit the body. You need to know the benefits of long-term training on all of the body systems. This page focuses on the long-term effects of exercise on the skeletal system.

Your bones, exercise and health

The bones of the skeletal system benefit from taking part in weight-bearing activities over a period of time, or activities where your body works against resistance.

Weight-bearing activities are those that force your body to work **against gravity**. They do **not** include those where your body is supported, such as cycling or rowing.

Weight-bearing activities lead to:

↓

Increased bone density. Increased bone density means:

↓

Stronger bones. Stronger bones mean:

↓

Less chance of breaks/fractures. Less chance of osteoporosis.

Impact of long-term training

The impact of these benefits on performance is:

- there is an increased ability to withstand force, leading to improved performance
- the performer is less likely to have time out from training due to injury, also leading to improved performance.

Regular exercise also leads to:

↓

Stronger ligaments and tendons. Stronger ligaments mean:

↓

Better support of joints to increase stability. More stability means:

↓

Less likely to dislocate a joint. Less likely to get an overuse injury (if tendon).

Golden rule

Remember to break down your thoughts into clear stages:

- effects (what happens)
- benefits (how this helps the performer)
- impact (how that helps the performance).

Worked example

(a) State the difference between weight-bearing activities and non-weight-bearing activities. **(1 mark)**

(b) Explain why weight-bearing activities are beneficial to the skeletal system. **(2 marks)**

(a) Weight-bearing activities make your body work against gravity – in other words, you have to support your own body weight – whereas non-weight-bearing means you have help supporting your body weight, like sitting in a boat.

(b) Weight-bearing activities increase bone density, leading to stronger bones, so there is a reduced chance of osteoporosis.

← It is important to understand the term 'weight-bearing', as this can bring about adaptation to the skeletal system.

Now try this

Using an example, explain why stronger ligaments will be beneficial to a rugby player. **(2 marks)**

Adaptations to the muscular system

You need to know the long-term effects and benefits of aerobic and anaerobic training and exercise on the muscular system.

Training adaptations

All performers will benefit from adaptations to the muscular system. However, it is important that the adaptations are appropriate for the activity.

Adaptations to the muscular system can be:

aerobic – due to regular aerobic activities, for example:

- games activities
- low-weight high-reps weight training

anaerobic – due to anaerobic activities, for example:

- sprinting
- high-weight few-reps weight training.

MON	TUE	WED	THU	FRI	SAT	SUN
Train	Rest day	Train	Rest day	Light training	Match	Rest day

As well as applying the principles of training, there must be enough time for rest and recovery between training sessions for adaptations to take place and to prevent overtraining.

Effects and benefits of aerobic adaptations include:

- **hypertrophy** of slow twitch muscle fibres – benefits activities where muscular endurance is required
- increased myoglobin content – improves oxygen supply to muscles
- increased size of mitochondria; increased number of mitochondria – produces more energy aerobically.

Effects and benefits of anaerobic adaptations include:

- hypertrophy of fast twitch muscle fibres – benefits activities where strength and power are required
- **increased strength** – increases the amount of force that can be applied
- **increased tolerance to lactic acid** – reduces muscle fatigue, so delaying the need to reduce intensity of work.

Key terms for the muscular system

- **Anaerobic** – without oxygen.
- **Aerobic** – with oxygen.
- **Hypertrophy** – increased size of muscles.
- **Myoglobin** – oxygen stores in muscles.
- **Mitochondria** – where energy is produced using oxygen.

Worked example

Which of the following is an anaerobic adaptation of the muscular system? **(1 mark)**

☒ **A** Increased tolerance to lactic acid
☐ **B** Increased myoglobin content
☐ **C** Hypertrophy of slow twitch muscle fibres
☐ **D** Increased size of mitochondria

Now try this

Lucy exercises regularly to increase her fitness.

Describe **one** way in which the muscular system is affected by regular exercise and the long-term benefit of this effect on the performer.

(2 marks)

Adaptations to the cardiovascular system 1

You need to understand the effects of regular exercise on the cardiovascular system and how these adaptations benefit the performer. Some of these are described below.

Benefits of regular aerobic exercise

Regular **aerobic** exercise will lead to adaptations of the cardiovascular system. These adaptations make improvements to the system so it works more efficiently and benefits both health and fitness.

Health benefits include:

- reduced chance of a stroke
- reduced chance of coronary heart disease
- reduced chance of type II diabetes.

Golden rules

- 'Regular' means more than once a week over a number of weeks.
- It takes time for adaptations to take place and reversibility will occur if activity reduces or stops.
- Adequate **rest periods** are essential to allow these adaptations to occur.

What are the adaptations?

The adaptations to the cardiovascular system include:

- increased elasticity of the muscular wall of veins and arteries
- increase in size and strength of the heart (cardiac hypertrophy)
- increase in **resting** stroke volume (amount of blood leaving the heart each beat at rest).

Why are they of benefit?

The benefits of these adaptations are:

- 👍 drop in **resting** blood pressure
- 👍 good for health as it reduces the chance of coronary heart disease (CHD)
- 👍 good for fitness as the heart can contract more forcefully
- 👍 more blood is ejected from the heart each beat at rest, so the heart does not need to beat as quickly to supply the required oxygen.

Golden rule

Make sure you say **resting** when referring to adaptations to stroke volume. Adaptations occur over a long time and must not be confused with immediate effects, where more blood is pumped out of the heart per beat due to increased demand for oxygen.

Golden rule

Make sure you say **resting** when referring to adaptations to blood pressure. A drop in blood pressure in general is not a long-term benefit.

Worked example

Make sure you give a long-term effect on the heart.

Ria plans to sustain her involvement in exercise and physical activity.
Identify one long-term effect of participation in exercise on Ria's heart. **(1 mark)**

Increased strength of the heart.

Now try this

Give a potential impact on health of having a stronger heart as a result of regular participation in physical activity. **(1 mark)**

Adaptations to the cardiovascular system 2

You need to understand the effects of regular exercise on the cardiovascular system and how these adaptations benefit the performer. Other long-term training effects are outlined below.

What are the adaptations?

The adaptations to the cardiovascular system include:

- lower **resting** heart rate
- increased **maximum** cardiac output during exercise
- increased capillarisation (the development of a capillary network)
- increased number of red blood cells
- faster return to resting heart rate.

Note the use of the terms 'resting' and 'maximum'.

Why are they of benefit?

The benefits of these adaptations are:

- 👍 greater training zone: with an increased stroke volume, the heart needs to beat less often to eject the same amount of blood (see page 51 for more on training zones)
- 👍 increased oxygen delivery to working muscles
- 👍 increased ability to carry oxygen to working muscles and increased rate of removal of carbon dioxide
- 👍 more efficient recovery after exercise.

Cardiac output and stroke volume

To increase cardiac output you can:

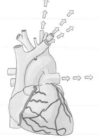
increase heart rate

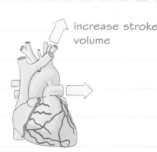
increase stroke volume

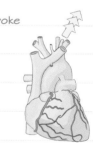
increase both heart rate and stroke volume

Cardiac output is the amount of blood leaving the heart per minute.

HR = heart beats per min.

SV = volume of blood leaving the heart per beat.

Worked example

One of the long-term adaptations of regular participation in physical activity is an increased number of red blood cells.

Explain the benefit of an increase in the number of red blood cells to a long-distance runner. **(3 marks)**

Long-distance running is an endurance activity. This type of running is aerobic and the increased number of red blood cells will help with an increase in transport of oxygen to the working muscles.

Credit is given for recognising the type of activity that requires oxygen.

Now try this

Regular participation in aerobic exercise will have an impact on the body systems.
State **three** of the effects of regular aerobic exercise on the cardiovascular system. **(3 marks)**

The effects and benefits of exercise to the respiratory system

You need to understand the long-term training effects of regular exercise on the respiratory system.

What are the adaptations?

The adaptations to the respiratory system include:

- increased number of alveoli
- increased strength of intercostal muscles
- increased strength of the diaphragm
- increased tidal volume (the amount of air you inspire or expire in a normal breath)
- increased vital capacity (the maximum amount of air your lungs can expire after the maximum amount that they can inspire).

Why are they of benefit?

The benefits of these adaptations are:

- 👍 more opportunity for gas exchange between the alveoli and the blood – more oxygen from alveoli to blood, and more carbon dioxide from blood to alveoli
- 👍 increased muscle efficiency means more space is created for the lungs to fully inflate
- 👍 an overall increase in lung volume so you can take in more air and extract oxygen more effectively.

Therefore as a result of regular training:
- 👍 more air can be breathed in
- 👍 more oxygen is extracted from the air breathed in ready for transport to the working muscles.

diaphragm   intercostal muscles

The diaphragm attaches to the lower ribs and the intercostal muscles are located between the ribs to help move the chest when breathing.

Worked example

Which of the following is a long-term effect of participation in exercise and physical activity on the respiratory system? **(1 mark)**

- ☐ **A** Increase in blood flow to the lungs
- ☐ **B** Increase in oxygen debt
- ☒ **C** Increase in vital capacity
- ☐ **D** Increase in breathing rate

Option A relates to the cardiovascular system, not the respiratory system.
Options B and D are immediate effects of exercise.

Now try this

Briefly explain the impact of an increase in total lung capacity as a result of regular participation in physical activity on an individual. **(2 marks)**

Injury prevention 1

Many physical activities have risks associated with them that can result in injury. To prevent injury you need to be able to identify risks and know how to reduce them.

General and specific risks

- There are **general risks** associated with most physical activity. For example, you could sprain an ankle or pull a muscle in most activities.

- There are also **activity-specific risks**. For example, the risk of being hit with a hockey stick is specific to hockey.

You need to be able to identify and reduce all these risks. To do this:

1. Make a list of all the possible things that could happen in an activity.

2. Decide on a way of reducing each of the risks.

Example – hockey

Look at these examples of risks associated with playing hockey.

1. Heart attack
2. Shin splints
3. Pulled muscle
4. Fractured shin
5. Broken tooth

Each of these risks can be reduced through **personal readiness**.

Injury prevention through personal readiness

State how you would reduce each risk (risk reduction measure):

1. Complete a PARQ.
2. Allow recovery time.
3. Warm up.
4. Use the correct clothing.
5. Apply the rules of the game correctly when you are playing.
6. Use correct equipment (e.g. the right weight shot put for your age).

Then explain **how** each risk reduction measure will reduce the risk:

1. Identify any potential health risks and limit participation accordingly.
2. Prevent overuse injury.
3. Increase elasticity of muscle.
4. Wear shin pads to provide padding.
5. Don't lift hockey stick above shoulder so teeth are not hit.
6. Muscles can cope with the workload and don't strain.

 Worked example

Which of the following statements gives the **most** important reason for wearing the correct clothing when taking part in physical activity? **(1 mark)**

☐ **A** It gives you the opportunity to look good

☐ **B** It gives you a psychological advantage over the opposition

☒ **C** It reduces the chance of injury

☐ **D** It is in the rules of physical activity

Always watch for the word 'most'. Other statements may be true but are not the **most** important.

 Now try this

Complete the table below by giving examples of how personal readiness can reduce each potential sports injury. Use a different example for each one. **(2 marks)**

Potential sports injury	Example of risk reduction through personal readiness
Fractured shin	
Soft tissue injury	

Injury prevention 2

As well as checking personal readiness for an activity, there are other measures that should be taken to prevent injury.

Identifying risks in sport

If you consider the risks associated with rugby, you might identify the following as possible injuries:

- crush injury
- dislocated shoulder
- gash on leg.

Sometimes questions state an activity and ask you to identify the risks – but other times you are asked to choose the activity. If you are, make sure you choose an activity that has obvious risks. For example, it's easier to talk about risks associated with rugby than table tennis.

Here are **other measures** you could use to reduce the three rugby risks identified above.

✓ Make sure the competition is balanced. ➡

✓ Check the equipment.

✓ Check the facilities.

✓ Apply the principles of training, for example, progressive overload.

Here are examples of **how** each measure could be used to reduce the risk.

- Avoid having 18-year-old boys playing against 12-year-old boys. The younger (smaller) boys could get crushed in tackles as other bigger players land on them.
- Have padding around the posts to soften the impact in the event of a collision.
- Remove obstacles from the pitch (for example, broken glass) to avoid cuts.
- Ensure increase in training intensity is gradual, to avoid overuse and muscle injuries.

Identify other measures

If you are asked to identify other measures you can take to reduce risk, be careful to take them from different categories. For example, avoid having two ways of balancing competition, such as boys vs girls or black belt vs green belt in judo.

Have padding around the posts.

 Worked example

'Balanced' in this context is to do with evening out the sides, not remaining steady.

Complete the table below by stating how the competition has been balanced. **(4 marks)**

Competition	How competition has been balanced
Under 19 football tournament	Same age playing against each other
Women's indoor hockey championship	Same sex playing against each other
Judo brown belt competition	Same level competing against each other
Heavyweight boxing competition	Same weight category against each other

---

 Now try this

It is important that Lucy does not over-exercise as this may lead to injury.
State four other different ways that Lucy may avoid injury.

(4 marks)

Fractures

Unfortunately, even with every attempt to avoid it (see pages 65 and 66), injury can still happen. You need to know the common injuries that can occur when taking part in sport.

Fracture is the correct term for a broken bone.

Fractures happen when the force on the bone is stronger than the bone itself.

There are different types of fracture that can occur, including:

- compound
- simple
- greenstick
- stress.

Symptoms of a fracture may include:

- pain
- misshapen limb
- bruising
- swelling.

> When asked to give two different injuries do not say 'break' and 'fracture' – they are the same thing!

Types of fracture

- Compound, or open fractures, are where the broken bone causes the skin to break, adding an additional complication of possible infection.
- Simple, or closed fractures, are where the bone does not break the skin.
- Greenstick fractures are common in younger children. This is where the bone bends on one side and breaks on the other.
- Stress fractures are injuries commonly caused through overuse. This is where a small crack forms in the bone.

Fracture treatment

Bones will mend but they need to be treated by a doctor, who will make sure the bone is properly aligned and immobilised (usually by a plaster cast or splint) until it has healed.

  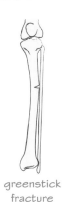

| simple fracture | compound fracture | stress fracture | greenstick fracture |

Worked example

Give an example of how a fracture might occur in the following activities. **(2 marks)**

(a) Rugby: Fracture to the leg when landing awkwardly in a tackle.

(b) Cycling: Falling off a bike and putting your arm out to break your fall could cause a fracture of one of the bones of the wrist, arm or shoulder.

> This question is asking for the practical application of fractures to physical activities.

Now try this

Describe **two** named types of fracture. **(4 marks)**

Concussion and dislocation

Two common injuries that occur when taking part in sport are concussion and dislocations. You need to know what they are and how taking part in sport and physical activity could cause them.

Concussion

Concussion is a **mild head/brain injury**. It is caused by a blow to the head or by whiplash (sudden and severe movement of the head) shaking the brain inside the skull.

This type of injury is **common in contact sports** such as:

- rugby, where there can be a clash of heads or a sudden impact with the ground
- cycling, where falling off the bike may lead to a bang on the head.

Symptoms of concussion may include:

- confusion
- dizziness
- unconsciousness
- nausea.

Treatment: seek medical advice and monitor closely to make sure the symptoms do not get worse. Rest.

Dislocation

Dislocations can be very painful. It is where one of the bones at a joint comes out of place. For example, a dislocated shoulder is when the bone in the upper arm comes away from the shoulder socket.

Dislocations are often caused by a fall or blow to the area. For example, falling when running and putting out your arms to save yourself can result in a dislocation at the shoulder.

Symptoms of a dislocation may include:

- pain
- misshapen joint
- swelling.

Treatment: RICE (rest, ice, compression, elevation – see page 70) can be used as a temporary measure for dislocations. However, because of possible damage to surrounding nerves and tissue, it is essential to seek medical help for dislocations as soon as possible.

Worked example

Most injuries have specific symptoms. Select **two** symptoms of a dislocation from the boxes below and enter them in the spaces provided.   **(2 marks)**

Swelling	Bleeding	Dizziness
Confusion	Misshapen joint	

Swelling

Misshapen joint

Always select the most obvious choices. Although some confusion might occur if in pain, it is not the **most** obvious choice for a dislocation, so can be ruled out along with bleeding and dizziness.

Now try this

Describe a common cause of concussion and suggest a way to avoid it.   **(2 marks)**

Injuries at joints and soft tissue

Other common sports-related injuries include injuries at a joint, for example, torn cartilage and soft tissue injuries. You need to know about these types of injuries and suitable treatments for them.

Torn cartilage

Cartilage acts as a cushion at the end of the bones. **Torn cartilage** is an injury at a joint where small tears appear in the cartilage. It is a common injury in many sports.

A mis-timed or bad tackle in football can cause a torn cartilage injury.

Examples of how torn cartilage can occur include:

- forceful twisting
- sudden impact/stopping.

Symptoms of torn cartilage include:

- pain
- swelling
- stiffness at the joint restricting movement.

Treatment: rest and strengthening exercises.

Sprain

A **sprain** is an injury at a joint where some of the fibres of the ligament are torn.

It happens when the joint goes through a greater range of movement than normal, tearing some of the fibres. This type of injury is common in many sports.

A sprain could be caused by a sudden change of direction to dodge an opponent in netball.

Examples of how sprains can occur include:

- forceful twisting
- overstretching the joint.

Symptoms of a sprain include:

- pain   • bruising   • swelling.

Treatment: RICE (rest, ice, compression, elevation – see page 70).

Soft tissue injuries

As you have seen, some injuries are to the bone such as fractures, and some are to the tissue surrounding the joints such as sprains and torn cartilage. There are also injuries that are specifically classified as soft tissue injuries:

- strain (see page 70)
- tennis elbow (see page 70)
- golfer's elbow (see page 70)
- abrasions.

Abrasions

Abrasions are minor injuries to the skin such as:

- a graze   • a cut.

These can occur in any activity due to a knock or fall.

Treatment: abrasions must be cleaned and covered with a sterile dressing. Pressure should be applied to stop blood flow.

Worked example

What type of injury is a twisted ankle?   **(1 mark)**

☐ **A** Fracture
☐ **B** Deep bruising
☐ **C** Strain
☒ **D** Sprain

Now try this

For a named sport, describe how a sprain could occur whilst playing that sport.   **(1 mark)**

Remember: you can **strain** a muscle or you can **sprain** a joint. You need to be clear which is which.

Soft tissue injuries and RICE

There are a number of different types of soft tissue injuries that you need to be familiar with.

Tennis elbow

Tennis elbow is a joint injury where the tendons are inflamed. Pain is felt on the **outside** of the elbow.

Tennis elbow can be caused by poor technique or overuse. For example, repetitive use when playing a backhand in tennis can damage the tendons, resulting in tennis elbow. It can also be caused by activities other than tennis, for example, golf or badminton.

Golfer's elbow

Golfer's elbow is another joint injury where the tendons are inflamed. Pain is felt on the **inside** of the elbow.

Golfer's elbow can be caused by poor technique or overuse, for example, excessive practice of a particular shot on a driving range without appropriate rest.

Other activities such as throwing can also result in golfer's elbow.

The importance of rest and recovery

Notice how overuse is often the cause of injuries to the muscular-skeletal system. This is why it is so important to include rest as part of your training schedule, so that recovery can take place.

Strains

Strains are a stretch or tear in the muscle. Sometimes this is known as a **pulled muscle**. Strains occur due to overstretching.

Symptoms of strains include:

- swelling
- pain
- bruising.

Treatment: RICE (see below).

Golden rule

Completing a warm up can help reduce the chance of strains occurring.

Treatment

The most appropriate treatment depends on the severity of the injury. More severe injuries will need further medical attention. However, a common treatment for joint injuries to reduce the swelling and pain is known as RICE.

RICE

Rest	Do not use the injured area, allowing time to heal and to prevent further damage.
Ice	The cold from the ice will help reduce swelling and pain. (Should not be in direct contact with the skin and not left for too long.)
Compression	Apply a bandage to the area to help reduce swelling and provide support (make sure the bandage is not too tight).
Elevation	Keep the affected area raised to help reduce swelling.

Now try this

Describe a common cause of golfer's elbow and tennis elbow, and suggest a way to avoid these injuries. **(2 marks)**

Remember to put the components of RICE in the correct order.

Anabolic steroids

You need to know about performance-enhancing drugs (PEDs) and their effect on sporting performance and performer lifestyle. PEDs are banned as there are dangerous side effects and they can improve performance artificially. The World Anti-Doping Agency (WADA) is responsible for testing for PEDs. Anabolic steroids are one type of PED.

Many types of anabolic steroids have the same chemical structure as the male hormone testosterone. This is produced naturally by the body, but performers increase the amount they have by taking artificially-produced versions of it.

To allow them to train harder for longer, so increasing **power** and **strength**.

To increase protein synthesis, helping to develop lean muscle mass.

Reasons athletes take anabolic steroids

To speed up recovery time.

To increase their chances of winning.

Due to pressure from others.

Health risk and cheating

There are lots of good reasons **not** to take performance-enhancing drugs. Using performance-enhancing drugs in competition is **cheating**.

Reported side effects of anabolic steroids include:

- liver damage and CHD
- testicular atrophy, which leads to a decrease in sperm count (infertility)
- skin problems, including acne
- mood swings, including increased aggression
- premature baldness.

Who might use anabolic steroids?

Anabolic steroids could provide an advantage in activities requiring **power**, like sprinting or weight lifting.

Sprinter Tyson Gay was banned from competing in 2013 after testing positive for anabolic steroids.

Rank these performers in order, so that the one most likely to use anabolic steroids is listed first, the one least likely is listed last. **(1 mark)**
- Tennis player
- Long-distance runner
- Sprinter

Sprinter, tennis player, long-distance runner

This rank order is based on the relative importance of power and strength to each of the performers. The more important they are, the more 'attractive' taking steroids becomes.

Remember to give two health risks. Some students missed out because they gave one health risk. Make sure you answer the question.

Identify **two** possible health risks of taking anabolic steroids. **(2 marks)**

Beta blockers

You need to know about performance-enhancing drugs (PEDs) and their positive and negative effects on sporting performance and performer lifestyle. Beta blockers are one type of PED.

Beta blockers are drugs that are designed to treat various health issues, particularly those associated with the heart such as high blood pressure. They work by blocking the effects of adrenaline, so helping slow down the heart rate.

They have a calming effect.

Reasons performers might take beta blockers

They reduce the performer's anxiety.

They reduce muscle tremor or shaking.

They allow the performer to remain in control.

They increase the chances of winning.

Health risks associated with beta blockers

Reported side effects of beta blockers include:

- slowing heart rate (therefore oxygen delivery, therefore drop in performance in endurance events)
- lowering of blood pressure
- sleep disturbance leading to tiredness.

As beta blockers work with chemicals that occur naturally within the body and they are quickly absorbed, it can be hard to detect them when testing for banned drugs.

Who might use beta blockers?

Use of beta blockers could be an advantage in any activity that depends on **precision**, for example:

- archery
- gymnastics
- target shooting
- diving.

Worked example

Which of the following is a known effect of beta blockers on health? **(1 mark)**

☐ **A** Nausea and vomiting   ☒ **C** Tiredness

☐ **B** Dehydration   ☐ **D** Loss of balance

Now try this

Some participants take illegal performance-enhancing drugs to control their heart rate, despite the obvious health risks. What effect do beta blockers have on a participant's heart rate? **(1 mark)**

Make sure you read the question carefully. This question asks about the effect on heart rate, so make sure you mention what happens to heart rate in your response.

Diuretics

You need to know about performance-enhancing drugs (PEDs) and their positive and negative effects on sporting performance and performer lifestyle. Diuretics are one type of PED.

Diuretics are drugs that increase the rate of urination, so increasing the amount of fluid the body loses. Unlike other performance-enhancing drugs, diuretics are banned not because they directly enhance performance, but because of other potential benefits.

To achieve quick weight loss (due to loss of fluid from the body).

Reasons performers might take diuretics

To mask or hide other performance-enhancing substances the performer may have taken, making them harder to detect.

Health risks associated with diuretics

Reported side effects of diuretics include:

- dehydration
- nausea, headaches
- heart / kidney failure.

Golden rule

If you are asked about the side effects of drugs, don't refer to 'heart problems' or 'kidney problems', as the use of the word 'problem' is too vague.

Who might use diuretics?

Diuretic use could be an advantage in any activity with a weight category or where it is a benefit to be light, for example:

- boxing
- horse racing (jockey).

It could also be useful to any performer trying to mask other performance-enhancing drugs.

Worked example

Give an example of a performer who may take diuretics in order to achieve quick (but temporary) weight loss. **(1 mark)**

Boxer

Boxers have to be within certain weight categories before they are allowed to compete.

EXAM ALERT!

Do give the obvious answer – make sure you focus on what's being asked and don't overcomplicate your answer.

Now try this

Which of these categories of drugs is used to hide the presence of other performance-enhancing drugs? **(1 mark)**

☐ **A** Anabolic steroids   ☐ **C** Diuretics

☐ **B** Stimulants   ☐ **D** Narcotic analgesics

You may be able to answer some multiple choice questions without looking at the options given. If you know the answer to the question without needing to look at the options, this is a good way of checking your answer.

Narcotic analgesics

You need to know about performance-enhancing drugs (PEDs) and their positive and negative effects on sporting performance and performer lifestyle. Narcotic analgesics are one type of PED.

Narcotic analgesics were designed to relieve pain temporarily. They act on the brain and spinal cord to dampen the effect of painful stimuli, thus masking pain.

They increase the performer's pain threshold.

They give a sense of euphoria.

Reasons performers might take narcotic analgesics

They mask injuries so the performer can continue to compete.

They give a sense of being invincible.

Health risks associated with narcotic analgesics

Reported side effects include:

- nausea / vomiting
- anxiety / depression
- kidney / liver damage
- addiction
- concentration loss
- further damage to injury (due to masking pain).

Who might use narcotic analgesics?

Activities where performers might risk using narcotic analgesics include:

- sprinting
- boxing
- football
- swimming.

In fact, **any** performer with an injury who wishes to carry on training and performing could be tempted to take this category of drug.

Worked example

When might a performer be tempted to take narcotic analgesics? **(1 mark)**

When they have an injury but need to continue to train.

Now try this

When injured, some performers may be tempted to take drugs to allow them to maintain their training.
What category of drug would a performer take to mask or hide pain? **(1 mark)**

Make sure you know the reasons why performers are tempted to take performance-enhancing drugs.

Peptide hormones

You need to know about performance-enhancing drugs (PEDs) and their positive and negative effects on sporting performance and performer lifestyle. Peptide hormones are a type of PED and are found naturally in the human body. Some performers are tempted to artificially increase the amount of these hormones to gain benefits.

Peptide hormones

There are **two** peptide hormones you need to know.

- **Erythropoietin (EPO)**
  EPO is one occasion where you can write an abbreviation in your exam paper!

- **Human growth hormones (HGH)**
  You will sometimes see the abbreviation HGH – this stands for human growth hormones.

Reasons performers might take peptide hormones

Erythropoietin (EPO) can:

- help increase red blood cell production, and therefore:
- increase oxygen delivery to working muscles.

Human growth hormones (HGH) can:

- help increase muscle mass and therefore strength
- burn more fat.

Health risks associated with peptide hormones

Reported side effects of peptide hormones include:

EPO

- increased thickness of the blood
- blood clots / strokes / deep vein thrombosis
- increased risk of heart attack.

HGH

- arthritis
- heart failure
- abnormal growth in feet and hands
- diabetes.

Who might use peptide hormones?

Activities where performers might risk using peptide hormones include:

EPO

Any activity where an increase in **oxygen** delivery would be helpful, for example:

- rugby
- distance running
- distance cycling.

HGH

Any activity where an increase in **strength** would be helpful, for example:

- sprinting
- weight lifting.

Worked example

In an attempt to improve performance, some participants will resort to taking performance-enhancing drugs. If a performer takes erythropoietin (EPO), what type of activity are they likely to compete in?   **(1 mark)**

An endurance event like long-distance running.

Now try this

Explain how erythropoietin (EPO) aids performance in long-distance runners.   **(3 marks)**

Stimulants

You need to know about performance-enhancing drugs (PEDs) and their positive and negative effects on sporting performance and performer lifestyle. Stimulants are one type of PED.

Stimulants are a category of drugs that temporarily elevate mood. They increase brain activity, making an individual feel more awake and alert, and as if they have more energy. The taking of stimulants in large enough quantities constitutes the use of performance-enhancing drugs and is therefore banned.

Reasons performers might take stimulants

To increase alertness (mental and physical) so the performer is quicker to respond.

To reduce tiredness.

To increase heart rate (and therefore oxygen delivery).

To increase competitiveness.

To increase levels of aggression.

Health risks associated with stimulants

Reported side effects of stimulants include:

- insomnia
- anxiety
- aggression
- heart rate irregularities.

Facts about stimulants

- Stimulants are found in everyday products that contain caffeine, for example, coffee and many soft drinks. However, you are unlikely to reach banned levels of caffeine simply through drinking these!
- Stimulants can be used to treat anything from a cold to ADHD.
- Amphetamines are one of the most common stimulants that are used illegally.

Who might use stimulants?

There are two main areas where stimulants might appeal to performers.

1. Where an increase in **aggression** would be helpful. It helps to have a certain level of aggression in very physical sports as the performer is more prepared to take the 'physical knocks', for example:
   - rugby
   - boxing
   - ice hockey.

2. Where the performer needs to stay **alert** over a long period of time, for example:
   - long-distance cycling
   - baseball.

 Worked example

Which of the following is a known effect of stimulants on health?   **(1 mark)**

☐ A Nausea and vomiting
☐ B Dehydration
☒ C Irregular and increased heart rate
☐ D Loss of balance

Consider all options and make sure your choice is the best from those available.

 Now try this

Describe the circumstances that might lead to a performer taking stimulants, even though they are a banned performance-enhancing drug.   **(2 marks)**

Blood doping

You need to know about the practice of blood doping, and its positive and negative effects on sporting performance and performer lifestyle.

Blood doping

Blood doping is different to taking performance-enhancing drugs (PEDs), as it is a method that is followed rather than something you take. It is a process some athletes will use to enhance their performance. This method, like PEDs, is banned from use in sport.

Blood doping is a process where performers have additional blood added to their bloodstream.

How is blood doping done?

Blood doping can be done in a number of ways, for example:

Using the performer's own blood

- The performer has his/her blood removed and stored.
- The body replaces the blood over a four to six week period.
- Prior to an event the blood that was removed is injected back in to the blood stream.

Using the blood of someone with the same blood type

- Blood is put into the performer's bloodstream via a blood transfusion.

Reasons performers dope

- Increase in red blood cells, therefore:
- Increase in oxygen-carrying capacity.

Health risks associated with blood doping

- Infection from equipment leading to blood poisoning.
- Increased thickness (viscosity) of the blood due to increased number of red blood cells, which could lead to blood clots.
- Deep vein thrombosis due to blood clots, leading to heart failure.
- Stroke as a result of blood clots.
- Diseases carried in body fluids, for example, HIV and hepatitis.

Who might use blood doping?

Any performer who takes part in an activity where an increase in **oxygen** delivery would be an advantage, such as:

- long-distance cyclists
- long-distance runners
- games players where the game can last hours.

Blood doping can benefit endurance athletes.

Use the number of marks available as a guide to the number of points you make.

In an attempt to improve performance, some participants will resort to blood doping. Explain the type of activity these performers are likely to compete in. **(3 marks)**

They are likely to take part in an endurance event such as long-distance running. This is because they are getting extra blood so they can carry more oxygen, which is required to produce energy aerobically, allowing them to maintain a higher level of performance for longer.

Now try this

Explain why blood doping might lead to infection. **(3 marks)**

Warm up

You need to know the phases, purpose and importance of a **warm up** and be able to give examples of the activities included. It is important to remember that a warm up will prepare you physically and mentally so you can perform at your best, but also helps prevent injury.

Warm ups

You must know:

- the three phases of a warm up
- the order in which they occur
- examples of activities at each stage
- the significance of each stage.

Phase 1 Pulse raiser

To raise the heart rate and speed up oxygen delivery. For example, jogging up and down the pitch.

Phase 2 Stretching

Stretching the muscles and soft tissues you are about to use increases their elasticity and range of movement. For example, hamstrings stretch.

Phase 3 Drills

These are more intense practices relating to the main session, such as dribbling if you are about to play basketball.

Golden rule

A good warm up should take a minimum of 10 minutes and probably much longer, as it gradually increases the intensity the muscles are required to work at.

Reasons for the warm up

The benefits of a good warm up are extensive.

 It physically and mentally prepares you for exercise.

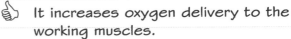 It increases oxygen delivery to the working muscles.

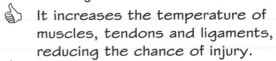 It increases the temperature of muscles, tendons and ligaments, reducing the chance of injury.

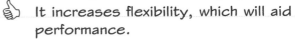 It increases flexibility, which will aid performance.

The drills you do should mimic those you are about to use in the main session, in order to:

- help prepare muscles
- focus your mind
- rehearse the skills you are about to use.

Practise the skills you will use in the game as part of your warm up.

Worked example

State three phases of a warm up. **(3 marks)**

1 Pulse raiser
2 Stretching
3 More intense exercise / drill related to the main session

EXAM ALERT!

Students sometimes get confused by the term 'phases'. Make sure you give the three different phases, rather than examples of them.

Now try this

Three of the following statements relate to warm ups and their purpose. Which statement does not? **(1 mark)**

☐ **A** The pulse raiser section of the warm up increases the amount of oxygen transported around the body

☐ **B** The warm up decreases the amount of lactic acid present and therefore reduces the likelihood of muscle soreness after the activity has finished

☐ **C** The warm up gets the performer mentally ready for the activity, as well as physically ready

☐ **D** The warm up increases the temperature of the body, resulting in it being better prepared for activity

Cool down

You need to know the phases, purpose and importance of a cool down and be able to give examples of the activities included.

Cool down

The purpose of a cool down is to return the body to its resting levels gradually, so there are no problems due to suddenly stopping exercise.

> ### Golden rule
> A cool down should **always** be completed after physical activity and sport.

Structure of a cool down

There are two stages of a cool down:

1 Light exercise, e.g. slow jogging – at a much lower intensity than you have just been working.

2 Stretching – stretch the muscles you have used in the main activity.

A cool down is **not** designed to prevent injury – you should not get injured at this stage as you have finished the main session and will be reducing the intensity of the work.

Reasons for the cool down

There are many benefits from a cool down:

- aids the removal of lactic acid, which can build up in the muscles making them feel stiff and sore
- aids the removal of carbon dioxide and other waste products
- helps bring the heart rate and breathing rate **slowly** back down to their resting rates
- helps avoid dizziness due to blood pooling in the lower limbs which can happen if you suddenly stop exercising
- improves flexibility.

Stretching after an activity, while the muscles are warm, helps to improve flexibility.

Option A isn't a benefit and is clearly incorrect; however, C and D could be thought correct if you only read the question quickly. Be careful to read all the words in each statement – the words underlined in C and D should show you these are incorrect answers.

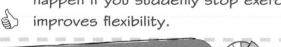
Worked example

Which of the following statements is a benefit of a cool down? **(1 mark)**

- ☐ **A** It increases lactic acid production
- ☒ **B** It reduces the risk of muscle stiffness after exercise
- ☐ **C** It <u>further</u> increases blood flow to the muscles after exercise
- ☐ **D** It reduces the chance of injury <u>during</u> the activity

EXAM ALERT!

Remember, you can cross through incorrect answers on the question paper as you work through the multiple choice questions.

Now try this

Choose words from the box below to complete the following statements about the cool down phase of an exercise session.

(6 marks)

This takes place .... exercise. It is made up of .... phases. To begin with, the performer might carry out some light .... followed by .... Effective cool downs can reduce muscle .... and increase muscle ....

> tension, after, strength, two, sprinting, during, four, skills, stretching, jogging, soreness, flexibility

Component 1 – Extended answer question 1

There will be 9-mark extended answer questions on each of your exam papers - one in the short course and two in the full course.

☑ demonstrate your knowledge and understanding of the topics related to the question
☑ apply the topics to relevant situations
☑ analyse and evaluate.

(See Exam skills pages 118–119 for more detail on answering extended answer questions.)

Worked example

Evaluate the extent to which a warm up is necessary for a hockey goalkeeper.   **(9 marks)**

The goalkeeper will complete a warm up before the match. They will complete a pulse raiser, such as jogging to the 23 metre line and back. This will raise the heart rate and get more oxygen to the working muscles so that energy is produced aerobically for the goalkeeper when they are constantly moving and getting into position to be ready to save any shot at goal.

The second phase of the warm up involves completing stretching exercises, stretching all the muscles the goalie is likely to use, for example, hamstrings and quadriceps stretches. Stretching will help increase the elasticity of the muscles, preventing a strain if the goalie overstretches when reaching out to prevent the ball going in the goal.

The final phase of the warm up is completing short drills, for example, saving shots at goal from various points around the 'D'. These help skills practice and mental focus, helping the keeper be alert and focused to save shots at goal in the match.

You could argue that a warm up is not important to a goalkeeper as they do not move as much as other players, and if they warm up they may just cool down again if not involved in play. However, it is still important, as once warm they would be ready for a sudden break at the start of the match, reducing risk of injury if they need to move at full stretch. Also psychologically they will be ready, confident in their ability to block the shot. Without a warm up they would not be physically or mentally ready to play at their best.

When answering this question you will be assessed on your ability to **link ideas together** to show your understanding of different topics when applied to sport and physical activity.

Evaluate

An evaluation requires you to review information and bring it together to make a judgement based on the information you have presented.

For each point you make you should **give information about the topic**. Here you can see there is general information about a warm up and the purpose of the three phases. This knowledge has then been applied by linking specific examples to a hockey goalkeeper.

Use paragraphs to separate your points clearly.

Finally the response should make **judgements**. In this example these are made at the end of the response and are based on the points made previously. The **impact** on goalkeeper performance is considered as part of the evaluation.

Now try this

Evaluate the importance of vascular shunting during a football match.   **(9 marks)**

Component 1 – Extended answer question 2

There will be two 9-mark extended answer questions on each of your exam papers. To gain all available marks you will need to:

- ✓ demonstrate your knowledge and understanding of the topics related to the question
- ✓ apply the topics to relevant situations
- ✓ analyse and evaluate.

(See Exam skills pages 118–119 for more detail on answering extended answer questions.)

Worked example

Evaluate the selection of the grip dynamometer test and the Harvard step test to test the fitness of a netball performer before planning her training programme. **(9 marks)**

Plan – talk about both tests, apply both tests to netball, evaluate if they are the right tests for this performer.

Fitness testing is useful before starting a training programme as it can identify strengths and weaknesses that could then be addressed in training.

The grip dynamometer test can be used to measure strength and the Harvard step test can measure cardiovascular fitness.

Both of these components of fitness are relevant to a netball player, as they need strong arms to ensure passes have enough force to get to their intended destination, and they need cardiovascular fitness so that they can keep playing for the whole match without tiring, meaning their performance would be better than someone with lower levels of cardiovascular fitness.

If the test results show that the levels of these two components need improving, the training programme can be designed to help. However, both tests have disadvantages. The grip dynamometer test only measures strength in the lower arm and hand, and if leg strength needs to be improved this would not be identified by this test. The Harvard step test is only 5 minutes long, whereas a game of netball is much longer. The player could consider the Cooper 12-minute run test as an alternative test as it last 12 minutes. Although this is still not as long as a match, it is longer and therefore should give a better idea of the player's level of cardiovascular fitness for netball.

> Look carefully at the question – the key word is **evaluate**, so you need to review the information you present. Fitness tests and netball are also mentioned, so you need to focus your response on these areas.

> It is always a good idea to complete a brief plan to help focus your thoughts.

> Start by demonstrating knowledge and understanding of the topics.

> Then make specific links by applying your knowledge to relevant question context.

> Finally, draw the information together to make judgements. Think of any negatives as well as the positives of the tests.

Now try this

When participating in some physical activities there is a high risk of injury.

Evaluate the need for injury prevention methods in **two** contrasting physical activities such as badminton and boxing. **(9 marks)**

Improving health

You need to understand that health can be promoted through participating in a well thought-out personal exercise programme (PEP).

The health benefits of training

Health is defined as:

- a state of complete **emotional**, **physical** and **social** wellbeing, and not merely the absence of disease and infirmity.

Regular training, with the correct application of the principles of training, will increase fitness. Through that training, all three aspects of health can be improved.

Planning a training programme

Personal health can be improved through an appropriate training programme, but the training programme needs to be developed carefully to gain the benefits you want.

Training programmes require:

1 planning (aims and design)   **3** monitoring

2 developing   **4** evaluating.

Promoting personal health through a PEP

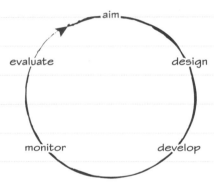

Your **health aim** would need to be clear; for example, 'to increase my cardiovascular health.'

A clear **aim** would allow you to create an appropriate PEP **design** through correct selection of training methods, for example, an aerobic training method to improve cardiovascular health.

Once underway, the PEP can be **developed**, for example, by refining activities so they continue to be appropriate to your aim, for example, increase training time by 5 minutes each session.

The PEP should also be **monitored**, so that adjustments can be made, for example, an increase in intensity when the work load becomes easy.

Finally, the PEP should be **evaluated** regularly, so that it or the aims can be modified, for example, a new aim if the previous one was met or training adapted if the aim is not being met.

Worked example

Why is it important to monitor your progress whilst completing a personal exercise programme to improve your health? **(3 marks)**

In case there is a problem with your design. If there is, you will need to modify the programme, otherwise you will not get the health gains you were expecting.

Although reference is made to a PEP, questions in Component 2 will focus on health and lifestyle. For this paper you just need to understand the process of PEP development to bring about health gains.

Now try this

Explain, using an example, how developing a PEP can promote personal health.   **(3 marks)**

Physical health

You need to know how increasing physical ability, through improving components of fitness, can improve **physical** health and reduce health risks, and how these health benefits are achieved.

Physical health benefits

Improvements in physical health result from regular exercise.

The health benefits include:

 stronger bones / **reduced** chance of developing osteoporosis

 reduced chance of coronary heart disease (CHD)

reduced chance of a stroke

reduced chance of obesity.

The improvements are achieved by:

* taking part in weight-bearing activities like running and walking
* reducing cholesterol / lowering blood pressure
* reducing cholesterol / lowering blood pressure
* burning excess calories while exercising.

The impacts of exercise on health and performance

It is the **end result** that brings the health benefit. For example, one health benefit from taking part in regular exercise is a reduced chance of coronary heart disease (CHD). This is as a result of lower cholesterol levels.

So, just stating 'lower cholesterol' would not be enough – you would need to say the **impact** of this is a reduced chance of CHD.

> Remember, weight loss is only a health benefit if you are overweight. Losing weight if underweight will damage your health.

In addition to the general improvements in **physical** health, you should be able to link these to improved performance:

* If blood vessels are not restricted due to high cholesterol, you would be able to continue to work harder as oxygen delivery would be improved.
* By being the right weight, that is not overfat, you won't be slowed down by excess weight from additional fat, therefore you will be able to perform for longer.

Negative effects of training on physical health

As well as the many positive effects of training on physical health and performance, there are also some **negative effects**. These include:

 overexertion leading to heart attack or stroke

 overuse injuries – for example, if you have a strain you may not be able to take part in physical activity for several weeks

 less effective immune system – for example, if you have a cold you may have to work at a lower intensity because oxygen delivery is reduced, therefore energy production will also be reduced.

Worked example

Which of the following statements describes a physical health benefit of exercise? **(1 mark)**

☐ **A** Meeting new people

☐ **B** Gaining an aesthetic appreciation of movement

☐ **C** Feeling better about body shape

☒ **D** Losing weight if overweight

Now try this

Use an example to explain how poor physical health can affect performance in physical activity. **(3 marks)**

> link your example of poor health to performance in sport or physical activity.

Emotional health

You need to know that in addition to improving physical health, regular physical activity can also improve emotional health.

Exercise and emotional health

The benefits of exercise to **emotional health** include:

👍 stress relief: helping to prevent stress-related illnesses such as depression

👍 competition

👍 reduced boredom

👍 aesthetic appreciation: aesthetic appreciation is recognising the beauty or skill of a movement. For example, you might enjoy seeing a football player demonstrate a high level of skill when they control the ball and kick a perfect volley.

The improvements are achieved by:

• taking your mind off of any problems
• causing an increase in serotonin (a chemical found in the body) – when it is released it makes you feel good
• having fun when you play
• feeling good if winning/meeting a challenge
• having something to do
• watching skilful performances.

Increase in self-confidence/self-esteem

Another emotional health benefit of exercise is an increase in self-confidence/self-esteem.

Confidence is increased **because**:

• you feel part of something
• you are performing better
• you think you look better.

Confidence is increased **by**:

• becoming a member of a team
• practising more
• losing weight due to exercise (if previously overweight).

Golden rule

You should always try to match a reason **why** something is achieved with an example of **how** it can be achieved. Always try to match a 'why' with a 'how'.

Negative effects of training on emotional health

As well as the many positive effects of training on emotional health, there are also some **negative effects**.

For example, training could lead to injury and if a performer cannot train this in itself can lead to depression.

Worked example

Physical activity can improve your emotional health by helping you 'feel good'. Which of the following causes this 'feel good factor'?   **(1 mark)**

☐ **A** An increase in testosterone
☒ **B** An increase in serotonin
☐ **C** An increase in blood pressure
☐ **D** An increase in narcotic analgesics

Now try this

One of the possible benefits of an active lifestyle is an increase in **self-esteem**. Using an example, explain how self-esteem can be increased through physical activity.   **(3 marks)**

Think about a specific aspect of playing sport and extend this example to make the link to how it can make you feel better about yourself.

Social health

It is important to be socially healthy as well as physically and emotionally healthy. Someone who is socially healthy can make friends easily and work well with others.

Friendships and social mixing

Joining a club or team is a great way to achieve the social benefits of exercise. These include:

- 👍 meeting new people and making new friends
- 👍 opportunities to get together with existing friends
- 👍 improving co-operation skills
- 👍 increased social activities (and therefore will not engage in antisocial behaviour).

Different age groups

Social benefits of an active lifestyle may well vary between different age groups.

For example:

- 👍 elderly person – getting together with friends as otherwise they may be lonely
- 👍 child – may see friends at school but needs to develop social skills.

Always be sure to relate your answer to a particular age range if asked to do so.

The importance of co-operating

Co-operation occurs when we work with others and demonstrate teamwork.

Improved co-operation can lead to better understanding of your teammates and better teamwork skills. This may make your team more successful.

Golden rule

Some words are similar, like co-operation, competition and co-ordination. Don't rush! Always read questions carefully to make sure you are thinking about the right one.

The negative effects of training on social health

As well as the many positive effects of training on **social** heath, there are some **negative** effects too.

For example, a negative effect of training could be that less time is spent with family and friends due to the large number of hours spent training. This could be due to the need to train to become an elite performer, or in some cases an obsession with training can occur.

Training could mean you spend less time with your family and friends.

Worked example

Shaznay has lost contact with a lot of her friends since leaving school. She has decided to join a local badminton club.

Explain how joining a club could improve Shaznay's social health. **(3 marks)**

If Shaznay has lost contact with friends, her social health could be negatively affected, as she doesn't have any friends to socialise with. By joining a club she has the chance to make new friends and is less likely to feel lonely, improving her social health.

The question asks you to **explain**. Notice how the first part of the answer identifies Shaznay's problem based on the scenario in the question, while the second part demonstrates **how** joining a sports club will help solve the problem.

Now try this

Think carefully about the category!

Enjoyment is an emotional benefit of participation in physical activity.
Explain how the social benefits of participation can lead to increased enjoyment. **(2 marks)**

Lifestyle choices 1

The choices you make about what you eat, whether you smoke or drink alcohol, how much you exercise, what work you do and for how long, and how much rest and sleep you make time for will all impact on your health and wellbeing.

Diet

Government guidelines state daily calorie intake should be:

* 2500 calories for men
* 2000 calories for women.

Do you:

* eat enough?
* consume more calories than you use?
* eat too much of one food type?
* have a healthy balanced **diet**?

Your **lifestyle choices** about what you eat could make the difference between being healthy or having serious health issues, and having enough energy to take part in physical activity or not.

Negative effects of poor dietary choices include:

* **Anorexia** (an eating disorder due to poor emotional health where a person keeps their body weight as low as possible) – impacts a person's ability to achieve sustained involvement in physical activity. If you have little energy or become too tired and weak to take part in physical activity, your fitness and performance levels will deteriorate.

* **Obesity** – impacts a person's ability to move due to excess weight. It can lead to potential joint and heart issues. (See page 89.)

* **Diseases caused by lack of nutrients** such as:

  * rickets (due to lack of vitamin D or calcium), which can result in weak bones

  * scurvy (due to lack of vitamin C), which can result in tiredness

  * osteoporosis (sometimes due to lack of calcium), which can lead to weak bones.

Activity level

Government guidelines recommend that 5 to 18-year-olds do one hour of exercise every day. Four days should be spent on cardiovascular work; three on improving muscle and bone strength.

Do you:

* sometimes take part in physical activity?
* never take part in physical activity?
* take part in regular activity?

Benefits of taking part in physical activity (see pages 60 to 64) include a reduced chance of CHD and osteoporosis.

Work/rest/sleep balance

Rest does not mean doing nothing – it is time to relax and have fun.

* Do you work too much?
* Do you have too little/too much rest?
* Do you have too little/too much sleep?
* Do you have a good balance between the amount you work, rest and sleep?

Do your lifestyle choices prevent you from getting the right balance of work, rest and sleep?

A lack of sleep can lead to tiredness, lack of concentration and irritability. Government guidelines recommend teenagers have 8 to 10 hours of sleep each night.

Worked example

Eddie is 16 and enjoys playing in the school football team. Explain why the government recommends that teenagers like Eddie have 8 to 10 hours sleep every night. **(3 marks)**

If Eddie didn't get enough sleep this may start to affect his enjoyment of sport, as he may be too tired to play at his best. He may also become irritable with his teammates, leading to conflicts within the group and a drop in performance levels. The body needs sleep to recover from the day; without enough sleep it will not fully recover.

Now try this

Briefly explain the lifestyle choices that would make it unlikely that an individual would become anorexic.

(2 marks)

Lifestyle choices 2

Recreational drugs are also a lifestyle choice. These drugs are taken for enjoyment rather than to enhance performance. They can be **addictive** and certainly **damage health**. The most commonly used recreational drugs are alcohol and nicotine (found in cigarettes).

Negative effects on health

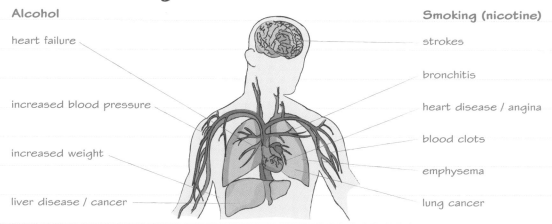

Alcohol

heart failure

increased blood pressure

increased weight

liver disease / cancer

Smoking (nicotine)

strokes

bronchitis

heart disease / angina

blood clots

emphysema

lung cancer

Negative effects on performance

Alcohol:

- Leads to slower reaction times.
- Makes the drinker less mobile due to excess weight.
- Causes loss of co-ordination.
- Causes loss of concentration.

These effects will have a negative impact on performance in **all** activities, whether aerobic or anaerobic.

Smoking (nicotine):

- Causes breathlessness.
- Reduces oxygen-carrying capacity.

These effects will have a negative impact on performance in **all** aerobic or endurance-based activities.

 Worked example

Smoking does not form part of a healthy lifestyle. Identify **two** of the possible negative effects of smoking on the cardiovascular system.   **(2 marks)**

Smoking can lead to heart attack or strokes.

Look out for questions where a specific area of health has been identified, in this case the cardiovascular system. Make sure you write about the correct system.

 Now try this

The question asks you to focus on the effects on the **respiratory** system.

Identify **two** of the possible negative effects of smoking on the respiratory system.   **(2 marks)**

Sedentary lifestyle

You need to know the consequences of a sedentary lifestyle on health.

A sedentary lifestyle

A sedentary lifestyle is a lifestyle where there is very limited or no physical activity.

More and more people have sedentary lifestyles due to advances in technology, as the requirement to be active has reduced. For example, rather than walking or cycling people use cars or public transport to get around. More and more jobs are computer based and therefore sedentary, for example, office work.

The lack of movement is made worse due to the amount of time spent sitting.

Too much sitting, not enough standing

Even if we are sedentary, research has shown that standing is a better alternative to sitting. It was reported that British people sit for nearly 9 hours (on average) a day.

- At school and work, large amounts of time are spent sitting down.
- At home, people spend many hours sitting watching TV or playing computer games.

There is even a campaign called 'Get Britain Standing', to help raise awareness of the need to avoid sitting for prolonged periods of time.

Examples of health risks due to a sedentary lifestyle	Examples of possible causes
Heart disease	Due to increased risk factors (high blood pressure, increased blood cholesterol)
Type 2 diabetes	There is an increased risk of diabetes due to being overweight
Obesity/excessive weight gain	Due to reduced metabolic rate and inactivity
Osteoporosis (weak/brittle bones)	Due to lack of weight-bearing activity
Loss of muscle tone and poor posture	Due to weak muscles
Poor fitness, e.g. lack of muscular endurance, strength, cardiovascular endurance	Due to lack of muscle use and muscular atrophy
Depression	Due to low self-esteem, due to being overweight, drop in brain function and low release of serotonin

Worked example

 Use of data

The graph shows the percentage of overweight children by age group over a 20-year period. Analyse the data to determine patterns in obesity levels. **(3 marks)**

11–15-year-olds have the highest obesity levels overall, and their percentage shows a continuing, although slight, upward trend. 6–10-year-olds showed a slight drop in obesity levels between 2012 and 2013, therefore there is a downward trend for this age group. This is good because in 1994 to 2003 the percentage increase for this age group matched the most overweight group, the 11–15-year-olds.

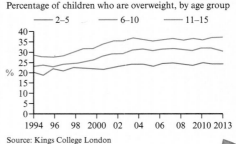

Percentage of children who are overweight, by age group
— 2–5   — 6–10   — 11–15
Source: Kings College London

All you need to know will be shown in the graph, so look carefully and say what you see.

Now try this

Remember to make one point and then expand on it rather than making three unrelated statements.

Give an example of a sedentary lifestyle choice and briefly explain a potential health problem due to this type of lifestyle. **(3 marks)**

Impact of a sedentary lifestyle on weight

There are specific excess-weight-related issues linked to having a sedentary lifestyle. You need to be aware of and use the terms overweight, overfat and obese. Remember, it is too vague to say someone is 'fat'.

Overweight

- The term 'overweight' means that you weigh more than the expected weight for your height and sex.

- You can be overweight while not being overfat.

- Being overweight is not in itself harmful – unless it is accompanied by also being overfat.

Some top performers will be overweight due to other factors, for example, muscle girth and bone density, but they do not have excess fat.

Overfat

The term 'overfat' means you have more body fat than you should have. If the level of fat in the body is excessive, it can lead to health problems, for example:

- high blood pressure
- high cholesterol levels.

Note that it is possible to be overfat but not actually be overweight.

Obese

'Obese' is a term used to describe people who are very overfat. This is where the body fat has increased to a level that is seriously unhealthy (not just being a few pounds overweight). High levels of excess fat can lead to:

- mobility issues / lack of flexibility
- additional stress on bones and joints
- heart disease
- type 2 diabetes
- depression due to low self-esteem.

The impact on sustained involvement

In addition to the serious health issues of being obese, overfat or very overweight, there will also be an impact on achieving sustained involvement in physical activity.

 Some of the resulting health problems, for example, heart disease, will prevent any strenuous physical activity.

 If you become too tired, immobile, or have difficulty in walking or running, this will affect your ability to take part in physical activity.

 Worked example

Explain the difference between being overfat and being overweight.   **(3 marks)**

Overfat means having more body fat than you should have; overweight means weighing more than you should. This could be due to being overfat or it could be due to additional muscle mass, therefore being overweight does not necessarily relate to having too much fat but being overfat does.

Now try this

1 Identify **two** physical health risks associated with being obese.   **(2 marks)**

2 Briefly explain **one** impact of being overfat on achieving sustained involvement in physical activity.   **(3 marks)**

Diet and energy balance

You need to know the nutritional requirements for a balanced diet to maintain a healthy lifestyle and optimise performance in physical activity and sport. You also need to know the correct energy balance to maintain a healthy weight.

Explaining a balanced diet

👍 A balanced diet means eating the right foods, in the right amounts. This will enable us to work and exercise properly.

👎 If we don't eat a variety of foods in the correct proportions, we will not get all of the **macronutrients** and **micronutrients** we need to make up a balanced diet. Insufficient nutrients can cause health issues, for example, anaemia, rickets and scurvy.

Golden rule

Diet is what we eat on a day-to-day basis and should not be confused with 'being on a diet'.

The Eatwell Guide

The Eatwell Guide shows how we need to make up our diet from different types of food to get the correct balance.

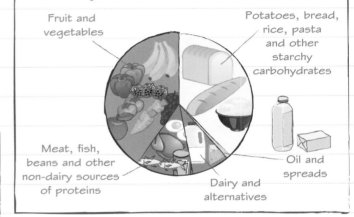

Fruit and vegetables

Potatoes, bread, rice, pasta and other starchy carbohydrates

Meat, fish, beans and other non-dairy sources of proteins

Oil and spreads

Dairy and alternatives

Variety as well as balance

You need a balance of food from the different groups and a variety from within each group.

For example, the Eatwell Guide shows we should have a high proportion of fruit and vegetables. The recommendation is that we eat 'between 5 and 10 a day', but variety within the group is still important to make sure we get the necessary range of nutrients. This is why eating 5 apples will only count as **one** of your '5 a day'.

The items we require fall in to the following seven areas:

- Carbohydrates
- Protein
- Vitamins
- Minerals
- Water
- Fibre
- Fats

The energy balance

The energy balance is making sure the **quantity** we take in relates to how much exercise we do.

- If we eat too much in relation to the amount of activity we do, we will become overweight.
- If we eat too little in relation to the amount of activity we do, we will become underweight.

We need to have a balance so we have the correct nutrients for energy.

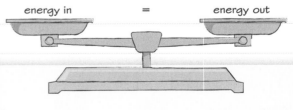

energy in   =   energy out

 Worked example

Valentin was trying to improve his diet, to make it more balanced. Define the term 'balanced diet'.

(2 marks)

A balanced diet means eating a variety of foods from all the different groups of food in the correct proportions.

 Now try this

Note this question is about health **not** fitness.

Diet is an important factor to consider when planning for a healthy, active lifestyle.
State **one** possible consequence of a poor diet on your health.

(1 mark)

Macronutrients

You need to know the role and importance of macronutrients for performers in physical activities and sports.

Macronutrients and why we need them

A nutrient is something that gives nourishment to the body. 'Macro' is the opposite of 'micro' and means things on a large scale. Macronutrients are the nutrients that we need to have in our diet in large quantities. We need them for **energy**, **growth** and **repair**. Everyone needs them, but those involved in physical activity will need more of them. There are three main types of macronutrients.

Carbohydrates

Fats

Proteins

- Contained in bread, pasta, potatoes, rice.
- Should be eaten in greater quantities than the other macronutrients.
- Provide us with energy for use in aerobic and anaerobic activity.

- Contained in butter, oil, fatty meats and fried food.
- Should form the smallest percentage of macronutrients in diet.
- Provide us with energy but should be eaten in moderation.
- Easily stored in the body and can lead to weight gain.

- Contained in cheese, milk, eggs, lean meat, fish.
- Used for growth and repair of the muscles.
- Can produce energy but this is not their main function.
- May be used by performers such as sprinters to aid muscle growth (hypertrophy).

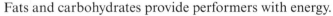

Worked example

Fats and carbohydrates provide performers with energy.

(a) Which macronutrient should you eat a larger amount of, fat or carbohydrate? **(1 mark)**

Carbohydrate

(b) Why is this food type a better source of energy for you? **(1 mark)**

It can be used in either aerobic or anaerobic activity.

EXAM ALERT!

Macronutrients and micronutrients are easily confused – learn these terms.

Think about what your body needs when you exercise.

Now try this

 1 Give **one** reason why you need to consider what you eat if you exercise regularly. **(1 mark)**

2 Explain the use of macronutrients in maintaining a healthy, active lifestyle. **(4 marks)**

Micronutrients

You need to know the role and importance of micronutrients for performers in physical activities and sports.

Micronutrients are the nutrients that we need to have in our diet in small quantities.

- Minerals and vitamins are micronutrients.
- We need them to maintain good health. Everyone needs them but those involved in physical activity will need more of them.
- Minerals and vitamins are found in the food we eat but some foods have more than others.
- Our body can store some for future use but some cannot be stored and so we need to eat a fresh supply every day.

Minerals and vitamins

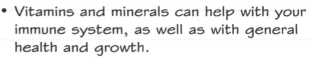

- There are many different vitamins and minerals.
- Each vitamin or mineral is good for different things. For example, you will often hear people talking about Vitamin C helping to keep you healthy and free from colds.
- Vitamins and minerals can help with your immune system, as well as with general health and growth.
- Vitamins are found in fresh fruit and vegetables.
- Minerals are found in lots of different foods, including meat and vegetables.

Specific micronutrients to note

Vitamin D
Vitamin D is found in dairy foods, such as milk, cheese and eggs, and helps the body absorb the mineral calcium.

Calcium
Calcium is a mineral found in foods such as milk and other dairy products. One of its functions is to help keep our bones strong.

Water and fibre

Water and fibre are not micronutrients, but they are still essential components of a balanced diet.

Water
Water prevents dehydration and is in most liquids and many foods.

Fibre
Fibre aids the digestive system and is found in foods such as cereals, vegetables and nuts.

Worked example

The following should all be present in a balanced diet. Which of them aids bone development?   (1 mark)

- ☐ **A** Fibre
- ☒ **B** Minerals
- ☐ **C** Carbohydrates
- ☐ **D** Proteins

> A specific mineral is not given, but it is the mineral calcium that aids bone development.

Now try this

The lists below give different combinations of important nutritional requirements of a balanced diet. Which of them does **not** include a micronutrient?   (1 mark)

- ☐ **A** Fibre, water, vitamin A, carbohydrates
- ☐ **B** Water, fibre, carbohydrates, fats
- ☐ **C** Carbohydrates, calcium, protein, fibre
- ☐ **D** Protein, fats, vitamin A, vitamin C

Optimum weight

You need to be able to outline why and how optimum weight varies and to explain how this may affect participation and performance in physical activity.

Optimum weight

Optimum weight is the ideal weight someone should be. An individual's weight will vary depending on their:

- bone structure
- height
- sex (male or female)
- muscle girth.

Bone structure

Some people have longer or wider bones than others and will also have greater bone density.

Someone with a larger bone structure will weigh more than someone of the same height with a smaller bone structure. Bone strength is important in many activities, in particular contact sports such as rugby.

Sex

Whether you are male or female can make a difference to your weight. Males tend to have more muscle mass and therefore weigh more. This provides men with an advantage in activities requiring strength or power. Males and females compete separately in activities of this sort, for example, athletics.

Muscle girth

This is the size of the muscle, its circumference. People with bigger muscles will weigh more. Bigger muscles are generally an advantage in activities requiring speed, power and strength, such as throwing a javelin.

Height

How tall you are will affect your weight – the taller you are, the more you may weigh.

Height can be an advantage in activities:

- where you need to outreach your opponent, for example, basketball
- when the use of longer levers may be beneficial, for example, bowling in cricket.

> ### Golden rule
> Suggested optimum weight should only be used as a guideline, as it will vary due to height, sex, bone structure and muscle girth.

Optimum weight will vary according to roles in specific physical activities and sports.

Many **elite** performers, for example, sprinters and rugby props, might be considered to be overweight because they are very heavy due to their muscle mass.

Jockeys and feather (minimum) weight boxers may be considered underweight.

However, they are all in fact the **optimum** weight for their sport.

Worked example

State **three** factors that will affect optimum weight. **(3 marks)**

1   The height of the individual: the taller they are the more they will weigh.
2   How much muscle they have: the greater their muscle girth the more they will weigh.
3   The sex of the individual: men tend to weigh more than women.

Now try this

State the impact of bone structure on optimum weight. **(1 mark)**

Dietary manipulation

As well as a balanced diet to maximise good health, what we eat can also improve performance in sport.

Dietary manipulation

In order to optimise performance, top performers will plan exactly what they eat and when they eat it to get the most advantage from the food they eat. This is known as **dietary manipulation**.

You need to know about:

- the timing of protein intake for power athletes
- carbohydrate loading for endurance athletes.

Protein intake

The timing of **protein intake** is important for power athletes, to maximise repair of muscle tissue broken down during explosive activity. In addition to rest and recovery, some performers take in protein as **soon as possible** after exercise to increase protein synthesis and therefore muscle growth.

This approach is used by:

- performers that work anaerobically, for example, sprinters
- hammer throwers
- power lifters.

Carbohydrate loading

This strategy increases the amount of carbohydrate stored as glycogen in the muscles, to provide energy for performance. The body can't store much carbohydrate, so unused carbohydrate is usually converted into fats and then stored. However, carbohydrate is a more quickly useable source of energy than fats.

Carbohydrate loading (see opposite) makes more energy from carbohydrate available for performers during activity. This method is used by endurance performers, for example:

- cross-country skiers   • marathon runners.
- triathletes

Carbohydrate loading

Depending on the type of carbohydrate loading this can be a few days or just prior to an event.

1 to 4 days before event:

- reduce amount of exercise
- eat a **high** carbohydrate diet
- reduce fibre intake

This leads to increased carbohydrate:

- therefore increase glycogen stores in the muscle
- allowing optimum performance for longer.

Hydration for physical activity and sport

When we sweat during physical activity we lose water and salt. It is vital that correct levels of these are maintained, as lack of fluid leads to dehydration causing:

- dizziness
- fatigue
- heat stroke
- increased heart rate.
- nausea
- muscle cramp
- thickening of blood

To help avoid dehydration and maintain hydration levels, you need to drink plenty of water or energy drinks:

- two hours before performance
- just before
- whenever possible during performance.

Performers drink water after activity to remain hydrated.

Now try this

Explain why a shot put athlete should think about their timing of protein intake.   **(3 marks)**

Classification of skills 1

Skills can be developed through practice. Understanding the different types of skill involved in a range of sports can help you determine the most appropriate strategies for improvement by identifying and using the best types of practice or guidance (see pages 97 to 102).

Classifying skills

Many different skills are used to take part in sport. If you know the **classification** of a skill, you can create an appropriate practice to improve it.

Some skills can be classified easily as they are at one end or the other of a **continuum**. However, many skills fall between the two ends of a continuum.

By thinking about the characteristics of each skill, you can place it at the right point along the continuum.

What is a continuum?

A continuum is a line that goes between two extremes. **Continua** means more than one continuum.

You need to classify skills on the following three continua:

open ———————— closed

basic ———————— complex
(simple)

low ———————— high
organisation   organisation

Open skills

Open skills are those that **are** affected by the surrounding environment.

Extreme 'open' skills (at the far open end of the open–closed continuum) need to be constantly adapted by the performer to meet the requirements of the activity as situations change around them. Examples include:

- a pass in hockey
- dribbling in football   • a rugby tackle.

To account for the opposition or positioning of team members, open skills need adapting as they are executed. For example, if a teammate moves further away from you, your lofted pass may need more weight. You adapt the skill to make sure your pass is still accurate and reaches your teammate.

With open skills, conditions are unstable and unlikely to be the same each time the skill is performed.

Closed skills

Closed skills are those that are **not** affected by the surrounding environment.

Extreme 'closed' skills (at the far closed end of the open–closed continuum) do not need to be adapted, because situations around the performer are stable. Examples include:

- a penalty kick in football
- a gymnastics vault
- a tennis serve.

Closed skills have a more set pattern and can be pre-planned. Although there can still be opponents, the opponents do not directly interact during the execution of the skill. This reduces the need to make sudden changes.

With closed skills, the conditions are likely to be the same each time the skill is performed.

Worked example

Sports are made up of a variety of skills. Place the three skills from football on the continuum.
(i) Goalkeeper saving a penalty   (ii) Forward taking a penalty   (iii) Midfielder dribbling the ball.   **(3 marks)**

open ●————————————————●————————————————————————————● closed
　　a midfielder　　　　　goalkeeper saving　　　　　　　　　forward taking
　　dribbling the ball　　　a penalty　　　　　　　　　　　　a penalty

Now try this

When asked to define there is no need to describe or explain – just say what it is.

Define the term open skill.

(1 mark)

Classification of skills 2

You also need to know about the basic (simple)–complex continuum, and the low organisation–high organisation continuum. Remember: skills can be classified on any of the continua.

Basic (simple) skills

Basic (simple) skills are those that:

- are simple
- require little thought
- do not need much information to be processed
- require little decision making.

Examples of skills at the extreme **basic** end of the continuum are:

- running
- cycling
- swimming
- chest pass.

Complex skills

Complex skills are those that:

- are difficult
- require thought and concentration
- require a lot of information to be processed
- require a lot of decision making.

Examples of skills at the extreme **complex** end of the continuum are:

- trying to dribble past defenders
- rock climbing
- passing the baton in a relay race
- a lay up in basketball.

basic ——————————————————— complex

Low organisation skills

Low organisation skills are those that:

- are easy to do
- have clear separate phases (making them easier to break down and practice).

Examples of skills at the extreme **low organisation** end of the continuum are:

- a tennis serve
- the triple jump in athletics.

High organisation skills

High organisation skills are those that:

- are harder to do
- have phases that are not clearly broken down without affecting the skill (making them harder to practice).

Examples of skills at the extreme **high organisation** end of the continuum are:

- tumbling in gymnastics
- a golf swing.

low organisation ——————————————————— high organisation

Worked example

Classify the following two football skills on a basic–complex continuum.

(a) Overhead kick   **(b)** Free kick   **(2 marks)**

basic ————————————————————————— complex
    free kick   overhead kick

Think about how much harder it is to complete an overhead kick than a free kick in football – the performer has a lot more to think about when executing the skill.

Now try this

State **two** reasons why a tumbling routine in gymnastics is considered a high organisation skill.   **(2 marks)**

Massed and distributed practice

Practice is needed to get better at a skill. It is also important that practice is structured so that it is effective. You need to be able to select the most relevant practice structure to develop a skill. This will depend on the performer's ability and the type of skill.

Massed practice

Massed practice is when there are little or no breaks in a session. The same skill is repeated over and over again, for example, 30 minutes of forehand drives in tennis.

👍 The correct movement pattern is grooved (getting the feel of the skill) so it is repeated next time.

👎 This type of practice can be boring.

👎 It can also be tiring, leading to errors and potentially accidents.

Massed practice is used:

- when the performer is:
  - experienced/skilled/motivated
  - older (less likely to get bored)
  - very fit
- when the skill is:
  - simple
  - low organisation
  - closed
  - not dangerous.

Example: a squash player continuously hitting forehand drives until they master the skill.

Distributed practice

Distributed practice is when there are breaks in the session providing rest periods or changes of activity. There are fewer repetitions and several skills can be practised rather than just one.

👍 The performer doesn't get too tired.

👍 It prevents boredom/keeps motivation high.

👎 The performer may not gain the skill in the time allowed, therefore taking longer to learn the skill.

Distributed practice is used:

- when the performer is:
  - a beginner/not very skilled
  - young (more likely to get bored)
  - not very fit
- when the skill is:
  - complex
  - high organisation
  - open
  - dangerous.

Example: five attempts at kicking the rugby ball at the posts, then rest and receive feedback from coach while another player has their turn.

Worked example

Identify the group that would be **most** likely to use massed practice.
(1 mark)

- ☐ **A** An adult group learning to abseil down a climbing wall
- ☐ **B** A group of Year 12 children learning back somersaults on a trampoline ✓
- ☒ **C** The school rugby first team doing passing drills
- ☐ **D** A 50+ return-to-hockey group

Although adults could use massed practice, the skill in option A is dangerous and the fitness levels of the group in option D may be low. The somersault skill in option B is also dangerous, therefore the school rugby team would be the most suitable for massed practice as they should be motivated and have good skill level.

Now try this

Explain the type of practice you would recommend for a group of 5-year-olds learning to play football. **(3 marks)**

Think about skill level and age group. Would you ask a group of 5-year-olds to repeatedly practice the same skill without a break?

Fixed and variable practice

Practice is needed to get better at a skill. It is important that practice is structured for it to be effective. You need to be able to select the most relevant practice structure to develop a skill. This will depend on the performer's ability and the type of skill.

Fixed practice

Fixed practice is when the whole movement of a skill is repeatedly practised in the same way so it becomes well learned.

The skill is not broken down in to smaller parts.

The golfers use fixed practice so their golf swing becomes well learned.

Fixed practice is used:

- when the sport is mainly made up of closed skills. The performer practices in a situation as similar to the performance situation as possible.

During fixed practice:

- the situation does not change
- the routine is repeated and 'grooved' until it becomes automatic
- the equipment stays the same.

Variable practice

Variable practice is when the same skill is repeated in different situations.

Learning the skills in different situations means that when different situations arise during performance, the performer already has experience of them.

Practising against an opponent makes sure the skill of passing is performed in slightly different ways.

Variable practice is used:

- when a sport is mainly made up of open skills because the situation is often changing.

The level of difficulty of the skill can be gradually increased so the performer becomes able to complete the same skill in more challenging situations.

For example, the performer could start by practising the skill in isolation, then bring in an opponent so it is a 1:1 situation, then bring in two opponents so it is 2:1. Each time the focus is on the same skill.

Worked example

Identify the skill that would be **most** suitable for using fixed practice. **(1 mark)**

☒ **A** Handstand on the beam in gymnastics
☐ **B** Dribbling the ball in hockey
☐ **C** Passing in wheelchair basketball
☐ **D** Handling the ball in rugby

A handstand is the most likely option, as the situation remains the same and would not need variable practice.

Now try this

Explain whether fixed or variable practice would be most suitable for developing the skill of passing in hockey. **(3 marks)**

Values of goal setting 1

You need to know the value of goal setting to improve and/or optimise performance in sport and physical activity. Remember that it is also important to **review** targets you have completed, so that you can see whether they were successful and use the results to set new targets.

Values of goal setting

Examples of the values of setting goals are:

Increased:

👍 motivation and feel-good factor

👍 focus

👍 standard.

Improved:

👍 monitoring of progress

👍 planning of training sessions (due to focus).

All these values can lead to improved performance.

SMART targets

In order for the goals you set to be successful, you need to use SMART targets. You need to apply all of them.

SMART stands for:

S = Specific

M = Measurable

A = Achievable

R = Realistic

T = Time bound

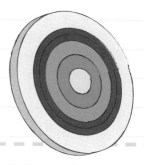

Specific ⓈMART

Description:

Your goal must be clear (specific).

Explanation:

A vague idea (for example, 'I must get better') is **not** specific or clear enough to provide the focus you need to bring about improved performance.

Application:

A specific and therefore clear target is:

To reduce the percentage of unforced errors in my passing from the centre third in netball.

Golden rule

Just saying 'to improve in netball' is too vague.

Measurable SⓂART

Description:

In order to know if your goal has been met successfully, it must be something that can be measured.

Explanation:

The best way to measure something is to have units of measurement, for example, time, distances, numbers. Then you can measure if the target has been achieved.

Application:

When giving examples of a measurable target make sure it has a number in it, for example:

To run 10 k **3 seconds** faster than my previous best.

Golden rule

Just saying 'to run a 10 k race faster' is too vague.

Worked example

Target setting should apply the SMART principle. State what the letter S in SMART represents and why it is important when setting targets. **(2 marks)**

The letter S stands for Specific – it is important to make sure that your target is clear so you know what you are aiming for.

Make sure you answer both parts of the question.

Now try this

State why targets should be measureable. **(1 mark)**

Values of goal setting 2

SMART targets must also be Achievable, Realistic and Time bound.

Achievable S M (A) R T

Description:

An achievable target means it is something that is possible for you to do.

Explanation:

You need to avoid setting targets which would be too difficult for someone to complete. This would be demotivating, therefore it is important that a performer has the ability, with training, to reach the targets set.

Application:

I currently run 100 m in 14.3 seconds. My goal is to run 100 m in 14.2 seconds.

Realistic S M A (R) T

Description:

A realistic goal is one that is possible, given all the factors involved.

Explanation:

Your goal might be achievable but are the other factors in place that make it realistic? For example, do you have access to training facilities, and do you have the time required?

Application:

I currently throw the javelin 30 m. I am going to start an additional training session each week and my goal is to throw 35 m by the end of this season.

Time bound S M A R (T)

Description:

Goals must be assigned a time frame for completion.

Explanation:

You need to have a cut-off point by which you should have achieved your goal, so that you can see if your training is having the effect you want.

Application:

My goal is to run 200 m in 45 seconds by 4 July this year.

Goals can be given a broad time line, which may be:

- short term
- medium term
- long term.

You may have several short-term goals which are leading towards a long-term goal.

For example:

My SMART goal is: I currently average a goal a match in hockey. With additional practice I aim to average 2 goals per match by 30 December.

Worked example

Targets for sports performers should be achievable and time bound. Complete the table below by describing:

- one consequence of setting unachievable goals. **(1 mark)**
- one advantage of setting goals that are time bound. **(1 mark)**

Consequence of setting unachievable goals	Performer would get demotivated and therefore stop training, causing a drop in performance rather than an increase
Advantage of setting goals that are time bound	Performer has a clear date to have achieved goal by so maintains motivation to complete it and beat the deadline

Now try this

Teachers will set targets with you to help you improve in all aspects of physical education. They will use the SMART principle to help you set effective targets.

The S of SMART stands for Specific, the M stands for Measurable and the T stands for Time bound.

What does the letter R of SMART stand for? **(1 mark)**

Visual and verbal guidance

Different types of guidance can be used to help performers improve. The type of guidance used depends on the skill and the ability of the performer. You need to know which type of guidance is most appropriate for different situations and know the advantages and disadvantages of each type.

Visual guidance

Visual guidance is when the performer is shown the skill. This can be done in a variety of ways, for example:

- a video of the performer
- pictures (e.g. photos or sketches)
- a good quality demonstration.

When using visual guidance:

- pictures must be clear (to enable understanding)
- demonstrations must be seen more than once (so the movement can be remembered)
- demonstrations must be good quality (so poor movement is not copied)
- demonstrations must be clearly visible.

Visual guidance is good for beginners so they can see what the skill should look like and create a mental image of what the movement should be.

It is also used when it is not possible to hear verbal guidance, for example, during play.

Advantages:

👍 can copy the movement

👍 can be done with groups.

Disadvantages:

👎 if demonstration is poor, incorrect movement can be learned

👎 time consuming/expensive if video used

👎 complex or quick movements are difficult to see clearly, so it can be difficult to recognise what the action is and to copy it.

Verbal guidance

Verbal guidance is when the performer is told information about how to complete the correct technique.

When using verbal guidance:

- the information must be clear (so the meaning is understood)
- the information must be concise (too much information can be confusing)
- the performer must be able to hear the instruction.

Verbal guidance is good for more experienced performers who know what the movement should look like and can make sense of the information. It is also used in situations where demonstrations are not possible, for example, during a break in play.

Advantages:

👍 instructions can be given quickly

👍 can be used during performance

👍 no equipment required.

Disadvantages:

👎 some movements are difficult to explain

👎 relies on the coach's communication skills being good enough that the performer can understand the information.

> ### Golden rule
>
> A combination of types of guidance can be used, for example, both visual and verbal guidance so the performer can see what the movement should look like while being told how to do it.

 Worked example

Give **one** disadvantage of verbal guidance. **(1 mark)**

Verbal guidance can be confusing if too much information is given.

 Now try this

During a coaching session the performers are shown a picture of how to hold a golf club. State the type of guidance being used and the likely level of ability of the group. **(2 marks)**

Manual and mechanical guidance

The two other types of guidance you need to know are manual and mechanical.

Manual guidance

Manual guidance is where the coach physically supports or moves the performer to help them get in to the correct position.

Examples include:

- a tennis coach holding a performer's racket arm and moving it through the correct range of motion for a forehand drive
- a trampoline coach supporting a front somersault.

Manual guidance: a gymnastics coach supporting a handstand.

Advantages of manual guidance:

👍 the performer can get a feel for the movement

👍 builds confidence

👍 can help break down a movement into phases.

Disadvantages of manual guidance:

👎 feeling is not the same as actually doing it unaided

👎 performer can become dependent on the support

👎 incorrect feel can lead to incorrect movement being learned

👎 can only be used 1:1.

Mechanical guidance

Mechanical guidance is where the coach uses equipment to support the performer to help them with the technique. For example:

- using a harness when learning somersaults in trampolining.

Mechanical guidance: using floats when learning leg movements in swimming.

Mechanical guidance can be used when the situation is dangerous.

Advantages:

👍 the performer can get a feel for the movement

👍 builds confidence

👍 reduces danger.

Disadvantages:

👎 feeling is not the same as actually doing it unaided

👎 performer can become dependent on the support.

👎 incorrect feel can lead to incorrect movement being learned

👎 cannot normally be used with large groups.

Worked example

Using an example, explain why mechanical guidance might lead to the performer becoming dependent on the support. **(3 marks)**

Mechanical guidance uses equipment; if a performer learns to swim using a float they may become reliant on it and not have the confidence to be in the water without the float.

Now try this

Which one uses manual guidance? **(1 mark)**

☐ **A** Performers are told how to complete the skill
☐ **B** Performers are shown how to complete the skill
☐ **C** Performers are supported completing the skill
☐ **D** Equipment is used to learn the skill

⬅ Remember **explain** means show your knowledge and understanding of the topic and then apply it.

Types of feedback

The ability of the performer and the type of skill will influence the type of feedback used.

Effective feedback

Feedback is used to:

- provide information about the skill being performed
- help improve skill
- reinforce good practice.

To be effective feedback must:

- not be too long – you can only process a small amount of information at a time
- be given as soon as possible – while the memory of the skill is still fresh
- be relevant to the performer – so it is specific for them and not the whole group.

Intrinsic feedback

Intrinsic feedback is from **within** the performer, for example, how the movement felt from feedback from the muscles. This type of feedback is important so performers can learn to spot their own errors.

Intrinsic feedback should be developed so the performer is not too reliant on others. Experienced performers use intrinsic feedback as:

- the skill is well learned
- they can feel their own errors and make amendments to their own performance based on their internal feedback.

Extrinsic feedback

Extrinsic feedback is feedback from **outside** the performer, for example, feedback from the coach telling you what you did right or wrong.

Extrinsic feedback is important, as someone watching the skill can observe problems and explain what needs to be done to correct them.

Less experienced performers are more likely to need extrinsic feedback, as they are not yet able to detect their own errors.

Concurrent feedback

Concurrent feedback is given **during** a performance.

Concurrent feedback can be intrinsic or extrinsic. For example:

- an experienced swimmer will feel if the turns are not going correctly and make adjustments for the next turn (intrinsic feedback)
- a coach can give a performer points to focus on while the performer is on the trampoline, such as 'point your toes', 'lift your arms higher' (extrinsic feedback).

Terminal feedback

Terminal feedback is given **after** the performance. Sometimes feedback cannot be given during a performance – this could be due to the rules or the skill not being suitable (for example, diving when the performer is underwater). To be effective, terminal feedback needs to be given as soon as possible after the completion of the skill.

Worked example

Explain why beginners would not be able to rely on intrinsic feedback when performing a skill. **(3 marks)**

A beginner will not have a clear idea of the skill they are trying to perform, therefore they will not be able to feel if they are doing the movement right or wrong, so they will need extrinsic feedback from a coach.

Now try this

The graph shows level of success at completing a skill over a number of attempts.

Analyse the graph to consider how feedback may account for the changing level of success. **(4 marks)**

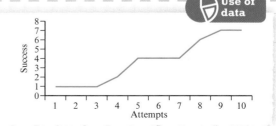

Mental rehearsal

You need to know about mental rehearsal – what it is and why performers use it as part of a warm up before physical activity.

Mental rehearsal

Mental rehearsal is a technique used by many elite performers. It involves mentally practising a skill or movement before physically doing it.

- During a warm up, you prepare physically and mentally for the coming activity. Mental preparation can be through mental rehearsal. (See page 78 for the phases of a warm up).

- During an event, the performer goes through a skill or sequence of events they are about to perform in their mind. This helps clarify the skill they are about to perform, so they are confident they are ready to perform.

Before participating in the Winter Olympics, this luge performer will mentally go through the race, visualising their route down the track **before** actually racing.

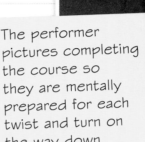

The performer pictures completing the course so they are mentally prepared for each twist and turn on the way down.

Although often completed before the start of a performance as part of a warm up, mental rehearsal can also be completed during a break or actually **during** a performance. For example:

- during a match when play is paused for a penalty kick in rugby, the performer will see themselves completing the skill well and the ball going between the posts before they take the kick. Having rehearsed a successful kick they then physically attempt it.

Time should be allowed specifically for mental rehearsal, as it can:

👍 be used to develop an existing skill

👍 help to focus the mind on the task

👍 reduce anxiety (due to focus)

👍 build confidence (due to mentally seeing successful performances).

Unlike physical practice, the outcome is always successful.

Worked example

Albert is competing in an important gymnastic competition. He completes his warm up but then has to wait before he can complete the vault. As he waits he starts to lose concentration and confidence, noticing the audience noise and worrying about the importance of this vault. Explain **one** technique Albert could use just before his vault to help regain confidence. **(3 marks)**

Albert could use mental rehearsal. Going through the vault he is about to do in his head will help him to focus and forget about the crowd. He will see himself doing the vault well, increasing his confidence.

Now try this

Say what you know about mental rehearsal and then apply this knowledge to the situation.

Before completing the high jump the performer uses the technique of mental rehearsal.
Briefly explain why this technique would be beneficial to him. **(3 marks)**

Socio-economic groups

Use of data You need to be able to tell the general trend in participation rates in sport and physical activity from any data that is provided and the impact on those participation rates based on the following personal factors: socio-economic group, gender, age, ethnicity and disability.

Participation rates

Sport England figures show that:

- some sports are more popular
- some groups of people are more likely to take part in physical activity.

Due to physical activity increasing our health, the UK government wants to encourage all groups to do at least a minimum amount of exercise. The government therefore tries to find ways to encourage participation for all.

Sport England and other organisations gather and analyse data to find out who participates in sport the most and why.

Data also shows that some groups are more likely to participate in particular types of activities based on the appeal of the activity.

You need to know some of the reasons for the different levels of participation and the barriers preventing everyone playing all sports.

Key terms

- **Participation rates** – the number of people taking part in physical activity.
- **Data** – facts and statistics gathered together to provide information that is easier to see.
- **Trends** – based on data, the general direction something is moving in (up, down or the same), for example, obesity levels in children.

Socio-economic group

Socio-economic groups split people according to their job or profession. The groups are given an order:

- Highest order – professional or managerial jobs where people have a lot of responsibility
- Lowest order – where there is no or limited responsibility.

Normally high-responsibility jobs are paid more, so these people have more money.

Socio-economic group can affect:

- participation rates
- the activity participated in.

Reasons for differences in participation include:

- **cost** – some activities cost more than others, for example, golf membership fees
- **availability** – some activities are harder to get to for some people than others, for example, skiing and rock climbing
- **time** – some activities take a long time and people have work and family commitments.

Worked example

Analyse the data to determine the trend in participation for the highest socio-economic group. **(1 mark)**

One session a week	(Oct 2005–Oct 2006)		(Oct 2010–Oct 2011)		(Apr 2012–Apr 2013)	
managerial/professional	40.1%	4,462,100	41.4%	4,812,000	41.3%	4,903,800
small employers/own account workers	32.4%	920,200	32.3%	958,400	32.7%	992,400
long-term unemployed	26.9%	3,450,200	26.6%	3,564,800	26.6%	3,639,900

Data from Sport England's Active People Survey on socio-economic groups.

The trend shows an increase in participation.

Now try this

 Do not be put off by 'data questions'. Say what you see.

Analyse the data in the table in the Worked example feature and explain the impact of socio-economic group on participation. **(4 marks)**

Gender and age groups

Use of data You need to be able to tell the general trend in participation rates in sport and physical activity from any data that is provided and the impact on those participation rates based on the following personal factors: socio-economic group, gender, age, ethnicity and disability.

Gender

Gender groups are determined by a person's sex, that is whether a person is male or female.

The reasons men and women participate more or less than each other can be due to the nature of the activity. Society still sees some sports as more associated with either men or women.

Lack of participation can be due to a number of different barriers preventing individuals from taking part.

Reasons for differences in participation include:

- **image** – some men do not want to do dance or play netball as they think these are 'female' activities, and some women would not play rugby or do boxing as they consider these to be 'male' activities. Either gender can worry about what other people think, preventing them from taking part
- **cost** – women generally earn less than men
- **time** – traditionally women will have restricted time as they spend more time looking after the home/children, as well as working, and so may have less time for sport.

Age

People are split into groups based on their **age**.

The reasons people from different age groups participate less than others can be due to the nature of the activity, but sometimes other barriers prevent them from taking part.

Reasons for differences include:

- **access** – a local tennis club may only allow juniors to play at weekends but if they have a weekend part-time job this means they cannot play
- **cost** – money may be needed to pay bills rather than pay for sport
- **time** – less time due to work
- **nature of activity** – depending on the individual, some activities may be more difficult to participate in as a person gets older. However, people in their 80s still run marathons!

Worked example

Use of data

According to Sport England's Active People Survey, during the period April 2012 to 2013, 54.7 per cent of 16–25 year olds played sport once a week, whereas 31.4 per cent of adults aged 26 years or older played sport once a week.

Give a reason for the different participation rates of the two age groups.   **(1 mark)**

Adults may have less time to take part due to work and family commitments.

Now try this

Use of data

This graph from Sport England's Active People Survey shows 'once a week participation by gender' in millions.

Identify the trend in participation rates for females between October 2011 and 2012.   **(1 mark)**

- Male (16+)
- Female (16+)

Male (16+): 7.78, 8.36, 8.52, 8.53, 8.57, 8.76, 8.76, 8.91, 8.75, 8.63

Female (16+): 6.30, 6.83, 6.75, 6.70, 6.54, 7.13, 7.08, 7.14, 6.96, 6.86

Millions (y-axis: 2 to 9)

| Oct-06 | Oct-08 | Oct-09 | Oct-10 | Oct-11 | Oct-12 | Oct-13 | Apr-13 | Oct-14 | Apr-15 |
| APS 1 | APS 2 | APS 3 | APS 4 | APS 5 | APS 6 | APS 7 | APS 8 | | |

Source: Sport England

Ethnicity and disability groups

You need to be able to tell the general trend in participation rates in sport and physical activity from any data that is provided and the impact on those participation rates based on the following personal factors: socio-economic group, gender, age, ethnicity and disability.

Ethnicity

People are grouped based on their culture or specific origin. We all have an **ethnic group**.

The reasons people from different ethnic groups participate more or less than other ethnic groups can be due to the nature of the activity, but sometimes other barriers prevent them from taking part.

Reasons for differences in participation include:

* **cultural influences** – family or peers influencing whether someone does or does not do an activity

* **stereotyping** – where people from particular backgrounds are steered towards or away from certain activities, e.g. people of African origin being associated with and encouraged to compete in long-distance running events, rather than activities such as swimming

* **cost** – due to socio-economic grouping, some people from different ethnic minority groups may have less money to spend on sport. For example, a Syrian refugee without a permanent job would not have the money needed to access more expensive sports.

Disability

A person's **disability** may influence their choice of activity.

There are many adapted activities available for people with disabilities, such as:

* wheelchair tennis and wheelchair rugby.

However, adapting sports can be expensive, and sports facilities able to run disability sessions may be limited. Therefore if a person's disability prevents them from joining in mainstream sport, there is likely to be limited access to participate.

Reasons for differences in participation include:

* **availability** – lack of facilities or clubs in the area

* **cost** – specialist equipment may be expensive

* **access** – physical barriers, such as a lack of ramps or pool hoists

* **stereotyping** – whether by the person with the disability (for example, thinking they are unable to participate) or by others (for example, assuming those with disabilities are unable to take part due to having a disability).

Worked example

Use of data

The following data is from the Sports Participation and Ethnicity in England National Survey 1999/2000. This survey gives the participation rates for cricket during this period:
Pakistani (10%), 'Black Other' (8%), and Indian (6%) men, which compares with the average for all men of 2%.
Explain **two** reasons for the different levels of participation between different ethnic groups. **(4 marks)**

The higher figures for the ethnic group 'Pakistani' could be due to stereotyping, where people have been encouraged to play cricket due to their ethnic origin or due to cultural influences where friends or family have introduced them to the sport.

> Think of a reason that could cause these differences in participation, e.g. stereotyping, and then and apply the reason to the given activity.

Now try this

Paul is a wheelchair user and wants to start to play wheelchair basketball. Describe a potential barrier Paul could face when taking up this sport.
(2 marks)

Commercialisation, the media and sport

You need to know about the relationship between commercialisation, the media and physical activity and sport: in other words, how they interlink.

The relationship between commercialisation, the media and physical activity and sport

This relationship is sometimes known as 'the golden triangle', because of the benefits each gives the others.

The interrelationship between commercialisation, the media and physical activity and sport is essential for each to maximise opportunity and profit.

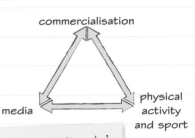

'The golden triangle'

Commercialisation

Commercial organisations are those that need to make a profit from the sale of goods, services or events.

These organisations can use sport and the media to get their product seen by millions, via advertising, sponsorship or endorsement.

Sponsorship can take many forms and it can be for:

- an individual (for example, golfer Rory McIlroy)
- a team (for example, Manchester United FC)
- an event (for example, Visa and the 2012 Olympics).

Media

The media provide entertainment. This can be live via TV, radio and the internet or reported after the event via newspapers and magazines.

The media need funding to provide entertainment, but commercial organisations are interested in using the media to promote their products as it can reach millions of people.

There are many media providers that are in competition with each other to gain the most viewers. The more viewers they have, the more likely they are to get funding from commercial organisations.

Physical activity and sport

The player/performer and the sport itself need funding for:

- facilities
- equipment
- competitions.

Both the media and commercialisation can help promote sport, and the media can also provide better opportunities for the spectator.

Worked example

Briefly explain why media providers, for example, Sky or BT Sport, fight to get exclusive rights to televise particular events. **(3 marks)**

Some events are very popular with viewers. Media companies want to be the only ones showing a popular event so that commercial organisations are interested in sponsoring the event or buying 'air time' to advertise their product, as they will be reaching a large number of people.

Now try this

State why commercial organisations, such as the company named on the advertising banners in the image, are interested in sponsoring events such as the Olympic Games. **(2 marks)**

The advantages of commercialisation

You need to know the **advantages** of commercialisation and the media for the **sponsor**, the **sport**, the **player/performer** and the **spectator**.

Advantages for the sponsor

👍 Excellent and relatively inexpensive advertising of their products, as:
- 👍 media can show products in advertisements during breaks in play
- 👍 brand names can be seen around venues and on performer's clothing during activity.

👍 Raised awareness of brands, leading to increased sales.

👍 Product associated with high-quality performance or health and fitness, giving brand high status.

👍 Increased media hype about an event = greater viewing numbers = more exposure for sponsor's products.

Advantages for the sport

More media coverage

⬇

Raised awareness of sports to help increase participation

⬇

Higher profile of sport = more commercial interest

⬇

Increased funding from sponsors, used to:
- 👍 run events
- 👍 develop grassroot to elite performers
- 👍 develop better facilities.

Advantages for the player/performer

👍 Can be paid millions to endorse products.

👍 Can train full-time and not have to complete another job to fund training, so can focus on becoming the best at their sport.

👍 Can receive top-quality products to use to help performance.

Advantages for the spectator

- 👍 More coverage.
- 👍 Top events.
- 👍 Replays.
- 👍 Red button choice.
- 👍 Player cam.
- 👍 Ability to buy the same clothes and equipment as role models.

Worked example

State **two** reasons why performers such as Lewis Hamilton (see photo) want sponsorship deals. **(2 marks)**

They will receive a large income from the sponsors in return for advertising their products.

They may also receive top-quality products that help their performance.

Formula 1 racing driver Lewis Hamilton is given as an example. Don't worry if you don't know the performer – think about general reasons why it would be good to get sponsorship.

Now try this

Identify why a sponsor would be interested in sponsoring a top performer such as Lewis Hamilton. **(2 marks)**

The disadvantages of commercialisation

You need to know the **disadvantages** of commercialisation and the media for the **sponsor**, the **sport**, the **player/performer** and the **spectator**.

Disadvantages for the sponsor

- 👎 The media may not get a high number of viewers.
- 👎 The company doesn't get the amount of exposure they wanted.
- 👎 The player/team doesn't perform well.
- 👎 A player becomes a bad role model – due to cheating, violence (in sport or out) infidelity, racism, etc. – sponsors become linked to these players and the product receives a negative image, making it less popular and reducing sales.

Disadvantages for the sport

- 👎 Clothing and rules changed to make the game more appealing to viewers.
- 👎 Fixture times and length of season changed to maximise viewing opportunities.
- 👎 Breaks in play for advertising purposes
- 👎 Minority sports not shown by media = decrease in participation.
- 👎 Minority sports get little media coverage and therefore lack sponsorship.
- 👎 Negative reporting can give the sport a bad reputation.

Disadvantages for the player/ performer

- 👎 Event times may make conditions less favourable for performers.
- 👎 Withdrawal of sponsorship can cause financial difficulties.
- 👎 Product may have a bad image (e.g. alcohol) or be unethical (e.g. child labour), giving a bad reputation to performer.
- 👎 Required appearances take time away from training.
- 👎 Pressure to win at all costs to keep sponsorship.
- 👎 Restricted to sponsorship clothing/equipment.
- 👎 No privacy.
- 👎 Negative reporting can lose sponsorship.

Disadvantages for the spectator

- 👎 High subscription cost for TV sports channels.
- 👎 Pay per view – need to pay again for certain matches/ events.
- 👎 High cost of merchandise.
- 👎 Minority sports not shown.
- 👎 Sponsors keep best tickets for hospitality reasons.

Worked example

Give reasons why the media dictating the start times of an event might be a disadvantage to the performers.

(3 marks)

The media will want the time of the event to be when most people are available to watch it. This may mean that it is during the hottest part of the day or in the evening, which may not be the ideal time for the performer to be at their best.

Now try this

Top cyclist Lance Armstrong (see image) admitted taking performance-enhancing drugs during his career. Briefly explain why this is a disadvantage to his sponsors.   **(3 marks)**

Sporting behaviour

Sport is meant to encourage fair play, honesty, discipline and teamwork. However, as sport becomes more important, not everyone demonstrates these values when they play. Two of the types of sporting behaviour you need to know about are sportsmanship and gamesmanship.

Sportsmanship

Sportsmanship is the type of behaviour that you **should** see in sport. It is where players display good conduct and do not resort to trying to win by unfair means.
For example:

- showing respect for officials and opponents
- shaking hands with opponents
- kicking the ball out of play if an opponent is injured
- being honest if the ball is out or if they break a rule.

Shaking hands before a match is considered a sign of good sportsmanship.

Sportsmanship creates:

- good role models
- a positive image of the sport or activity
- satisfaction/pride – you know you won honestly.

Gamesmanship

Gamesmanship is the type of behaviour that you **should not** see from performers in sport. It is bending (but not breaking) the rules to gain an unfair advantage.
For example:

- playing for time if winning
- entering a weaker team if the following match is more important
- sledging in cricket.

Sledging is when players verbally abuse their opponent to make them lose concentration and play badly.

Gamesmanship creates:

- bad role models
- a negative image of the sport or activity
- dissatisfaction – you know that you won due to an unfair advantage.

Worked example

State **one** reason why sportsmanship is a better behaviour than gamesmanship. **(2 marks)**

Sportsmanship is better as the players are not trying to win by gaining an unfair advantage, therefore they create a more positive image of their sport.

The question asks for one 'reason' why one is better than the other, so you don't need to explain that one **is** better than the other – you are told that in the question. Remember to use the number of marks available as a guide to how much information you need to give. In this answer, one piece of information is about sportsmanship and this is extended, giving the reason it is good for sporting image.

Now try this

The image shows a performer helping a member of the opposition who has cramp. Identify the sporting behaviour being shown. **(1 mark)**

To help remember which behaviour is which – 'a good sport' (as in sportsmanship) is good behaviour.

Deviance in sport

Unfortunately sometimes you see evidence of deviance in sport. You need to know the reasons why some performers resort to deviance at elite level and the consequences of this behaviour.

What is deviance in sport?

Deviance is **unacceptable** behaviour and is against the rules of sport. Examples of deviance include:

- cheating
- taking performance enhancing drugs
- violence (for example, biting)
- match fixing (for example, a goalkeeper deliberately letting in a goal to affect the score)
- racism
- sexism.

Why do some elite performers resort to deviance?

Even though it is against the rules, some elite performers use deviant behaviour to try to win by any means. Examples of why they do this are:

- for prizes
- for fame
- for sponsorship
- for money
- to get promotion to higher team
- due to pressure from coach/peers.

What are the consequences of deviance?

Deviant performers hope not to get caught, but there are consequences for breaking the rules. These range from fairly lenient, for example, a 'sin bin' (being sent off for a brief time) due to breaking a rule during play, to imprisonment for breaking a rule that is also against the law. Examples of consequences are:

- red card/being sent off
- fines
- banned from playing
- loss of sponsors
- loss of reputation/bad role model
- prison (for match fixing, illegal drugs, grievous bodily harm).

What is being done to try to prevent deviance?

Deviance is cheating and is unacceptable behaviour, so sporting organisations try to stop it and encourage fair play. Examples include:

- random drugs testing
- fair play awards:
  - UEFA Respect Fair Play rankings
  - FA Respect and Fair Play Awards
- campaigns, such as anti-drug (100% me), anti-racism (No to Racism, Show Racism the Red Card and Kick It Out).

> Think about the type of deviance and what the outcome of doing it is and therefore what could be the consequence of such an offence.

Worked example

Explain **one** consequence an elite performer could face if found guilty of match fixing. **(3 marks)**

They could get sent to prison for deliberately affecting the result as they (or others) could make money gambling on the outcome of the event.

Now try this

State, using an example, why an elite performer might resort to cheating despite the consequences if caught. **(2 marks)**

> Always remember to include an example if the question asks for one. Also, don't forget to tailor your answer to the question context. Try to use any images to help you — for example, why would drugs be linked to a gold medal?

Component 2 – Extended answer question 1

There will be two 9-mark extended answer questions on each of your exam papers (just one on the short course paper). To gain all available marks you will need to: **Short** **Full**

- ☑ demonstrate your knowledge and understanding of the topics related to the question
- ☑ apply the topics to relevant situations
- ☑ analyse and evaluate.

(See Exam skills pages 118–119 for more detail on answering extended answer questions.)

Worked example

Ms Harman is planning her after-school basketball practice sessions. One session is with the girls' first team and the other is a session with the new Year 7. She plans to focus on basic passing skills with the new students and free throws with the first team.

Discuss how Ms Harman should structure the practice sessions to develop these skills for both groups. **(9 marks)**

Ms Harman cannot use the same practice with both groups, as it would not be the best strategy as the groups are going to practice different skills and have different levels of ability.

There are several different ways to classify skill, for example, open or closed, where open skills are those affected by the environment and closed are not. Passing is an open skill. The Year 7s are going to work on their passing. This is an open skill, as during a match situation other players can try to take the ball from you or intercept it, therefore the Year 7s would need to adapt to the situation.

However, a free throw is a closed skill as it is not affected directly by others: an opponent cannot interfere with the shot, or when it is taken. It is always taken from the same point on the court.

There are different types of practice structure. Massed practice is when a skill is practised over and over without a break. Massed practice will be best for the first team as they are experienced and the skill is closed. As they are a little older and experienced they are likely to be motivated and able to repeat the skill to try to groove the correct movement pattern to improve the success of their free throws. Distributed practice would not give them time to groove the skill before moving on.

Distributed practice will be best for the new pupils as they are beginners and therefore they may not be able to repeat the skill over and over again. They also fairly young so would be likely to get bored with massed practice.

> When answering this question you will be assessed on your ability to link ideas together to show your understanding of different topics when applied to sport and physical activity.

> ### Discuss
> 'Discuss' requires you to give different or contrasting viewpoints, for example, the reasons why you would not do massed practice with beginners.

> For each point you make you should give information about the topic. Here you can see there is general information about skills and types of practice. This knowledge has then been applied by linking specific reasons to why the types of practice are relevant.

> Finally the response should make judgements. In this example reasons are given to support the selected practice structure, saying why it would be valid and also the disadvantages of another type of practice for that group.

Now try this

Short **Full**

Evaluate the relevance of the strategies of carbohydrate loading and the timing of protein intake for a long-distance cyclist.

(9 marks)

Component 2 – Extended answer question 2

There will be two 9-mark extended answer questions on each of your exam papers. To gain all available marks you will need to:

- ✓ demonstrate your knowledge and understanding of the topics related to the question
- ✓ apply the topics to relevant situations
- ✓ analyse and evaluate.

(See Exams pages 118–119 for more detail on answering extended answer questions.)

Worked example

Examine why an elite performer might resort to negative behaviours such as gamesmanship or deviance in their sport. **(9 marks)**

Gamesmanship is bending the rules without actually breaking them to gain an unfair advantage.

Deviance is breaking the rules in sport to gain an unfair advantage.

An example of gamesmanship is time wasting, for example, in tennis waiting until your opponent is about to serve and then stopping to tie your shoelace up. This is not actually cheating, but is bad sportsmanship and can be an effective way to break the rhythm of the server, disrupting their concentration in the hope they double fault.

An example of deviance is committing an act of violence, for example, in rugby deliberately stamping on an opponent's leg in a ruck to cause injury. This is cheating and is done to put a good player out of the game so the opponent's team stands less chance of winning.

Both gamesmanship and deviance are sometimes resorted to because the rewards of winning are so great. For example, the more you win, the better the media exposure you will receive. This may mean being selected for higher-paying clubs or increased sponsorship deals.

However, the consequences of cheating are great. Being seen deliberately breaking someone's leg would be reported as an act of deviance, and the performer's image would be badly affected, meaning they could lose sponsorship and face heavy fines or even imprisonment for grievous bodily harm.

When answering this question you will be assessed on your ability to link ideas together to show your understanding of different topics when applied to sport and physical activity.

Examine

'Examine' requires a justification or exemplification of a point based on analysis or evaluation – meaning make your point and build on it to make it clearer. This could be through examples, as shown here, and making a judgement about why people might be deviant in sport.

Knowledge and understanding of the topic are demonstrated through the points being made. This knowledge is then applied through examples leading to justifications – in this example why someone might be deviant.

Use paragraphs to clearly separate your points.

Now try this

Frankie joined a trampoline club. He is just starting to learn how to do back somersaults.
Evaluate the type of guidance the coach should use to help Frankie learn this technique. **(9 marks)**

Multiple choice questions

You will have two separate exam papers. You will have 1 hour 45 minutes to complete the question paper on Component 1, and 1 hour 15 minutes to complete the questions on Component 2. Both papers will contain multiple choice, short answer and extended answer questions. There will be eight multiple choice questions at the start of Paper 1 and six at the start of Paper 2. There is only one short course exam. The short course exam will contain seven multiple choice questions (MCQ).

Answering multiple choice questions

✓ Highlight the key words in the question.

✓ Read all the options carefully.

✓ Rule out the ones you know are wrong.

✓ Select what you think is the right answer.

✓ Double check the remaining options as well to make sure you are right.

Choosing the best answer

You need to be really careful when you are choosing your answer. There are often choices which look sensible, but aren't suitable for the **context** of the question. Always read the question carefully and choose the **most appropriate** option for the context.

Worked example

Nadine plays football. Which of the following nutrients should be consumed in the greatest quantities to provide her with the energy she needs to last the match? **(1 mark)**

☐ **A** Fats

☒ **B** Carbohydrates

☐ **C** Proteins

☐ **D** Minerals

This question is asking you to find the most relevant option for the football player. All of the options are nutrients that would be required however option D does not provide energy and can therefore be discounted. Of the remaining three options, fats should only be eaten in small quantities, and the main role of protein is for growth and repair of tissue. Carbohydrates provide energy and should be eaten in larger quantities than the other nutrients. Therefore option B is correct, as this is the only option that meets the requirements of the question.

This question is asking you to identify the muscle responsible for planter-flexion of the ankle at the start of the race.

We can discount options A and B as they are responsible for movement at the knee and hip. Option C and D do cause movement at the ankle however as muscles cause movement by pulling on the bone, if contraction of the tibialis anterior would pull the toes upwards, as this muscle is on the front of the lower leg therefore we can also discount option C.

Worked example

Identify which of the following muscles are used to planter-flex the ankle as the sprinter pushes against the blocks at the start of the race. **(1 mark)**

☐ **A** Quadriceps

☐ **B** Hamstrings

☒ **C** Gastrocnemius

☐ **D** Tibialis anterior

Short answer questions

Most questions will require you to write short answers. Some of these may only be one-word answers. Others will require a few short sentences or statements. Most short answer questions will be worth 1, 2, 3 or 4 marks.

Answering short answer questions

- ✓ Read the question carefully.
- ✓ Highlight or underline key words.
- ✓ Note the number of marks available for the question.
- ✓ Make sure you make the same number of statements as there are marks available. For example, if the question is worth 2 marks, make at least 2 statements.
- ✓ Don't repeat question words. If you do, make sure you go on to explain in further detail using other words too.

- ✓ If an activity is referred to in the question, make sure your answers relate to this activity.
- ✓ Give a range of answers rather than all from the same area (unless asked to do so). For example, if you are asked to give three examples of injury prevention, do not simply state three different safety rules, give a range of answers; for example, a specific safety rule, a named item of safety clothing and a specific item of safety equipment.
- ✓ Use the space available in the answer booklet as a guide. The space provided is plenty – be detailed but concise.

Describe vs explain

Different questions have different command words.

- If a question asks you to **describe** it is asking for a number of linked statements that give an account of something – you do not need to justify your statements.
- However, if you are asked to **explain** make sure you develop your answer, providing justifications for points that you make. You should be using words such as **because** or **therefore** to link statements, leading you to a more in-depth answer.

 Worked example

Explain why a high level of cardiovascular fitness is beneficial to a long-distance runner. **(2 marks)**

A high level of cardiovascular fitness is good for long-distance runners **because** they will get more oxygen transported to the working muscles, **therefore** they can use the oxygen to work aerobically and run at a faster pace for longer and improve their performance.

 Worked example

One of the possible benefits of exercise is an increase in self-esteem. Explain how self-esteem can be increased through physical activity. **(2 marks)**

Self-esteem is a form of self-confidence. It can be increased through physical activity because the more you practice a skill, the better you get at it, and being better at something makes you feel good about yourself, which increases your self-esteem.

Note how there are two parts to the answer. The first part explains the term and identifies something that would make you feel better about yourself (getting better). The second part gives a reason why this would increase self-esteem.

Use of data questions

Use of data — You need to be able to demonstrate an understanding of how data is collected. Data can be collected based on the quality of what you see e.g. how well a skill is performed (qualitative) or based on numbers, e.g. how many sits ups completed (quantitative). You may be asked to analyse data or to plot a graph. Use of data questions could be: multiple choice, short answer or extended answer. The short course exam will contain use of data questions.

Use of data

Some questions provide you with data and ask you to analyse it. This is not as hard as it sounds.

Data is just a way of presenting information to make it easier to use. For example, there is a lot of data in the table about three different individuals lifestyle choices.

To answer the question you just need to go through each set of choices and check to see if any would result in poor health.

Worked example

The table shows lifestyle choices of three different 16-year-old boys. Use the data to identify which boy has made the best lifestyle choices to maintain a good level of health. **(1 mark)**

Ahmed

	Smoker/ Non-smoker	Diet	Time spent training each week	Amount of sleep per night
Marvin	Non-smoker	Balanced diet	2 hours	6 hours
George	Smoker	Unhealthy diet	0 hours	4 hours
Ahmed	Non-smoker	Balanced diet	6 hours	8 hours

Trends

Some questions will ask you to interpret and analyse graphical representations of data and identify trends in the data.

Golden rule

A trend is just the general direction of a set of data; it could be increasing, decreasing or stable.

Worked example

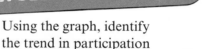

Using the graph, identify the trend in participation rates in the UK since 2006. **(1 mark)**

The overall trend is that there has been a rise in participation rates since 2006, although numbers have been dropping since October 2012.

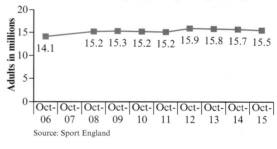

Once a week sport participation (millions)

14.1   15.2   15.3   15.2   15.2   15.9   15.8   15.7   15.5

Adults in millions

Oct-06 | Oct-07 | Oct-08 | Oct-09 | Oct-10 | Oct-11 | Oct-12 | Oct-13 | Oct-14 | Oct-15

Source: Sport England

Graphs and charts

You may need to present data.

- If the information you need to present is continuous, e.g. showing changes over time (recovery heart rate in minutes or participation rates in years), you should produce a line graph.

- If the information you need to present is for different categories of data, for example males and females or carbon dioxide and oxygen, you should produce a bar graph.

- If you are trying to compare parts of a whole then use a pie chart, e.g. the percentage of carbohydrate in your diet compared to other nutrients.

Worked example

Data shows 40.6% of men play sport at least once a week, compared to 30.7% of women. Complete the graph to show these participation rates. **(2 marks)**

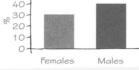

Current differences in sports participaion by gender

Females   Males

Use a bar chart, as the data is from two categories and is not over time.

Extended answer questions 1

There will be two 9-mark questions on each exam paper (just one on the short course paper). To answer these questions well you need to make sure you demonstrate: your knowledge of the topic in the question, and the ability to apply this knowledge and make a reasoned judgement. For example, if you are asked to evaluate two different training methods, by the end of your response it should be clear which of the training methods you think is best and why you think this.

✓ Take time to read the question carefully.

✓ Look for the key words in the question.

✓ Underline / highlight those words that tell you what you need to write about.

✓ Do not just write bullet points.

✓ Do not simply repeat the question words without explaining them.

Golden rule

It is a very good idea to do a quick plan before you write your extended answer to make sure you cover the key points.

Command words

The command words for the extended answer questions are likely to be one of the following:

- assess
- analyse
- discuss
- evaluate
- justify.

All of these words require a judgement as part of the response. (More details on the requirements for these words are explained in the Command words section on page 122.)

When writing your answers to the 9-mark questions, you need to plan to demonstrate three things:

1 Your **knowledge**.

2 Your ability to **apply** your knowledge.

3 Your ability to **evaluate** – to make a judgement about the things you have written.

Examples:

1 Naming or describing a method of training demonstrates **knowledge**.

2 Being able to link an appropriate method of training to a specific activity shows **application** of knowledge.

3 Being able to argue why one method of training is better than another for a particular performer demonstrates the ability to **evaluate**.

Key points to remember

For the extended answer questions, unlike other types of question, you do not get a mark for every point you make.

You are marked on your ability to:

- provide a full and balanced answer (which is why it is so important to identify the key words in a question)
- provide an answer which is well written and shows your full understanding of the topic in the question. Therefore, having identified the key words, it is essential that your response relates to all of them.

There is no one correct answer for the extended answer questions.

Extended answer questions can be based on any area of the specification.

The extended answer questions are designed to stretch you. A series of simple statements will not be enough for full marks.

Although you want to demonstrate knowledge application and your ability to evaluate, even if you can't do all of these things, make sure you **attempt** the question as any relevant content about the topic **will** gain some credit.

Golden rule

Always have a go!

Extended answer questions 2

Here is an example of an extended answer question, a possible answer and some notes to guide you.

Worked example

Penny is a 100-metre sprinter and runs for the county. Her friend Kam plays tennis for the county. Both need to work on their fitness for their sport.

With reference to the musculo-skeletal system, evaluate whether Penny and Kam should use weight training to improve their performance.   **(9 marks)**

The question asks you to **evaluate** therefore you need to make a decision based on whether you think Penny and Kam should use weight training. This decision should be based on the rest of your answer. Just saying 'yes' or 'no' will not gain credit!

Mentioning the benefits of weight training is a good way to start, as it shows your **knowledge** of the impact of the training method on one of the systems mentioned in the question.

Don't forget to demonstrate your knowledge across all aspects of the question; this means you need to talk about the skeletal system too. This part of the answer starts with **knowledge** then goes on to **application** of knowledge.

Weight training will increase both performers' muscular strength. The muscles will adapt and increase in size. Strength is a component of power. With an increase in strength it is possible to generate greater power, and this would be good for both performers. If Penny had more power she could apply more force to the track and therefore run faster in her event.

The skeletal system would become denser as a result of weight training, and the strength of bones and ligaments would increase improving joint stability. There would also be increased production of synovial fluid and overall flexibility.

These adaptations would benefit both performers. For example, Kam would be less likely to dislocate her shoulder when striking the ball and Penny would be less likely to suffer a hairline fracture during training, allowing her to continue to train and preventing reversibility.

By linking the adaptations from the training methods to the performers in the question, you are **applying** your knowledge.

If Kam increased her power she would be able to hit the ball harder so that her shots, for example her serve, would be harder to return.

One problem with an increase in muscle size is that the body becomes heavier (due to the extra muscle) meaning more energy is required to move the additional weight. This could have a negative effect on Kam, because if she becomes too muscular it will take more energy to move around the court and she will need to conserve her energy to last the whole match. Kam would be less reliant on power than Penny, as other factors are important in her game such as cardiovascular fitness and the skill to play the different shots, therefore while Kam may do weight training she would not wish to gain as much power as Penny.

Overall weight training would provide benefits for both performers and therefore could be added to their training schedule. However, it would not meet all of the performers' needs, therefore other training methods should also be included and in fact weight training should only be done in moderation for Kam.

Once you have made some points you can use these to support any **judgement** you make. For example, by identifying what is good about weight training for the performers, you are supporting the judgement that they *should* use this training method.

Glossary of key terms

The following list contains all relevant technical vocabulary, terminology and definitions associated with the content for Components 1 and 2. You will be expected to know and understand these, and other words and definitions, particularly for use in the exam papers. This glossary is not an exhaustive list of key terms and should be used in conjunction with the content for Components 1 and 2, to support your learning. Short course students only need to learn the terms relevant to the short course.

Aerobic work
Working at a moderate intensity so that the body has time to use oxygen for energy production, allowing the body to work for a continuous period (e.g. long-distance events, for the duration of a match)

Anaerobic work
Working at a high intensity without oxygen for energy production, therefore producing limited energy, so work period will be short (e.g. sprinting up the wing in a football match)

Antagonistic muscle pairs
Pairs of muscles that work together to bring about movement. As one muscle contracts (agonist), the other relaxes (antagonist) (e.g. the biceps and triceps: the triceps relax to allow the biceps to contract to flex the arm at the elbow; roles are reversed to extend the arm at the elbow)

Axis
A line around which the body/body part can turn

Basic skill
A simple skill requiring little concentration to execute

Closed skill
A skill performed in a predictable environment (e.g. a player taking a penalty)

Complex skill
A skill requiring a lot of attention/concentration

Deviance
Behaviour that goes against the moral values or laws of the sport

Distributed practice
Skill practice with intervals within a training session for rest or mental rehearsal

Exercise
A form of physical activity done to maintain or improve health and/or fitness – not competitive sport

Energy balance
Balance between energy input (via food) and energy expenditure. For body weight to remain constant, they must be equal

Feedback
Information received during or after a performance about the performance

Fitness
The ability to meet the demands of the environment

Fixed practice
Repeatedly practising a whole skill within a training session

Frontal axis
Imaginary line passing horizontally through the body from left to right, which allows flexion and extension

Frontal plane
Imaginary line dividing the body vertically from front to back (e.g. movement occurs in the frontal plane about the sagittal axis when performing a star jump)

Gamesmanship
Bending the rules/laws of a sport without actually breaking them

Guidance
Information to aid the learning of a skill. Can be given visually (e.g. through demonstrations); verbally (e.g. by the coach explaining how to perform the technique); manually (e.g. by physically moving a performer into the correct position); and mechanically (e.g. using a harness in trampolining)

Health
A state of complete emotional, physical and social wellbeing, and not merely the absence of disease and infirmity

High organisation skill
A skill that cannot be broken down easily and practised separately because the phases of the skill are closely linked (e.g. cartwheel, golf swing)

Hydration
The process by which water is ingested and absorbed into the body. Being hydrated means the body has the correct amount of water in cells, tissues and organs to function correctly. Note: average recommended daily intake = 2.5 litres water for men, 2 litres for women

Lactate accumulation
When lactate levels in the blood/muscle rise due to increased work intensity (e.g. moving from aerobic to anaerobic exercise)

Lactic acid
A by-product of energy production, formed when the body is exercising anaerobically at high intensity

Lever
A rigid bar that rotates around a fulcrum to apply a force to a load

Lifestyle choice
The choices we make about how we live and behave that impact on our health

Low organisation skill
A basic skill that can be broken down easily into different phases so each part can be practised separately (e.g. tennis serve, front crawl swimming stroke)

Macronutrient
A type of food required in relatively large amounts in the diet (e.g. carbohydrates, fats)

Massed practice
Practice that occurs without rest between trials

Mechanical advantage
Ability to allow a large load to be moved with a relatively small amount of muscular effort (characteristic of second class levers)

Mechanical disadvantage
Inability to allow a large load to be moved, except with a relatively large amount of muscular effort (characteristic of third class levers, which cannot lift as heavy loads, with the same amount of effort, as second class levers due to the position of the effort and load from the fulcrum)

Micronutrient
A type of food required in relatively small quantities in the diet (e.g. vitamins, minerals)

Muscle fibre types
Muscle fibres make up the skeletal muscle. The different fibre types are type I, type IIa and type IIx

Open skill
Skill performed in an unpredictable environment where the performer has to react and adjust due to the changing nature of the situation (e.g. a player trying to pass the ball to a teammate who is trying to get free of the opposition)

Optimum weight
The weight someone should be, on average, based on their sex, height, bone structure and muscle girth

Sagittal axis
Imaginary line passing horizontally through the body from front to back, which allows abduction and adduction

Sagittal plane
Imaginary line dividing the body vertically into left and right sides

Sedentary lifestyle
Where there is little, irregular or no physical activity

Sportsmanship
Qualities of fairness, following the rules and being gracious in defeat or victory

Transverse plane
Imaginary line dividing the body horizontally from front to back

Type I muscle fibres
Slow twitch muscle fibres, suited to low intensity aerobic work (e.g. marathon running) as they can be used for a long period of time without fatiguing

Type IIa muscle fibres
Fast twitch muscle fibres used in anaerobic work, which can be improved through endurance training to increase their resistance to fatigue

Type IIx muscle fibres
Previously known as type IIb muscle fibres. Fast twitch muscle fibres used in anaerobic work (e.g. 100-metre sprint), which can generate much greater force than the other fibre types but fatigue quickly

Variable practice
A training session that includes frequent changes of task so that the skill can be repeated in different situations

Vascular shunting
Process that increases blood flow to active areas during exercise by diverting blood away from inactive areas, achieved by vasoconstriction and vasodilation

Vasoconstriction
Narrowing of the internal diameter (lumen) of the blood vessel to decrease blood flow

Vasodilation
Widening of the internal diameter (lumen) of the blood vessel to allow increased blood flow

Vertical axis
Imaginary line passing vertically through the body, which allows rotation of the body in an upright position

Command words

A list of all the command words and their definitions that may appear in the exam papers for Components 1 and 2 is given below. Any of these command words could also be used in the short course exam.

Assess
Requires reasoned argument of factors to reach a judgement regarding their importance/relevance to the question context. For example, 'Assess the relative importance of...'

Analyse
Break something down into its component parts. This could be in relation to movement analysis

Calculate
Requires computation in relation to fitness data

Classify
Requires grouping or placing on a scale based on characteristics/analysis of characteristics

Complete
Requires adding information based on a stimulus/resource. This could be to complete a table, graph, chart or missing word/phrase from a sentence/statement

Define
Requires giving the meaning or definition of a word/term

Describe
Account of something without reasons. Statements in the response need to be linked. For example, 'Describe the lever system operating at the elbow...'

Discuss
Requires exploration of the issue/situation/problem that is being assessed in the question context, articulating different or contrasting viewpoints, for example, advantages and disadvantages

Examine
Requires a justification/exemplification of a point based on some analysis or evaluation within the response. For example, 'Examine the role of the first class lever system...'

Explain
Requires a justification/exemplification of a point. The answer must contain some linked reasoning. For example, the format of the response may be 'fact... because... therefore...'

Evaluate
Review/analyse information, bringing it together to form a conclusion/judgement based on strengths/weaknesses, alternatives, relevant data or information. Come to a supported judgement of a subject's qualities and relation to its context

Give
Generally involves the recall of a fact, or an example based on the given stimulus. For example, 'Give an example of a specific sporting movement...' Can be synonymous with identify/state

Identify
Can require a selection from a given stimulus or resource. For example, an option from a multiple choice question or analysis of data from source material such as a graph, or can be synonymous with give/state

Justify
Give reasons for answers. This could be a single response to extended writing answers depending on question context. For example, 'Justify the use of interval training to improve...'

Label
Requires addition of named structures or features to a diagram

Predict
Make a judgement about what is likely to happen in the future; normally associated with data questions.

Select
Requires a choice based on an evaluation of information from a given stimulus/resource

State
Generally involves the recall of a fact. For example, 'State **one** benefit of exercise...'. But can, when used in relation to a context, be used to determine your grasp of information presented. For example, a data analysis question. Can be synonymous with give/identify

Using an example
Often used with explain or describe where it requires an example to exemplify the point(s) being made

Which
Mainly used in multiple choice questions where a selection from a set of options is required. For example, 'Which **one** of the following...'

Key term
- **Synonymous** – in this context means 'can be used instead of'.

Answers

The following pages contain examples of answers that could be made to the 'Now try this' questions throughout the Revision Guide. In many cases these are not the only correct answers.

1. Functions of the skeleton
The skeleton is made up of joints, and movement occurs at these joints. **(1)** The skeleton also provides a place for muscle attachment, allowing movement. **(1)**

2. Classification of bones
The bones of the wrist are short bones. **(1)** These are very strong **(1)**, therefore they can take the weight of the gymnast and allow them to hold the handstand. **(1)**

3. Structure of the skeleton
Carpals/metacarpals/phalanges **(2 marks for any two)**

4. Classification of joints
A Ball and socket **(1)**

5. Movement at joints 1
Flexion **(1)**

6. Movement at joints 2
Abduction to adduction **(1)**

7. Movement at joints 3
Plantar-flexion is occurring at the ankle. **(1)** This will allow the volleyball player to use her toes to push off from the floor to gain greater height. **(1)**

8. Ligaments, tendons and muscle types
The main difference in characteristics is that voluntary muscles work under our conscious control, so we have to think about using them **(1)**, whereas cardiac muscle contracts unconsciously, therefore we have no knowledge or need to tell the heart to contract. **(1)** This is because we need the heart to pump continuously to transport blood and nutrients to the body otherwise we would die, so it continues to beat without us having to think about it. **(1)** However, we only need the skeletal muscles to work when we need specific actions. **(1)**

9. Muscles
Shoulder abduction **(1)**; example: preparation phase of an overarm throw in cricket. **(1)**

10. Antagonistic muscle pairs: biceps and triceps
The triceps is the agonist when the goalkeeper extends his arm at the elbow **(1)** and the biceps is the antagonist. **(1)**

11. Antagonistic muscle pairs: quadriceps and hamstrings
Quadriceps **(1)**

12. Antagonistic muscle pairs: gastrocnemius and tibialis anterior
Tibialis anterior **(1)**

13. Antagonistic muscle pairs: hip flexors and gluteus maximus
Hip flexors **(1)** Hip flexion **(1)**

14. Muscle fibre types
Type IIx muscle fibres have very high force of contraction **(1)** so a basketball player can produce enough power to jump high to intercept a shot. **(1)**

15. Cardiovascular system 1
Blood vessels close to the skin's surface vasoconstrict **(1)** to reduce the amount of warm blood going to the surface of the skin and heat being lost by radiation. **(1)**

16. Cardiovascular system 2
Right atrium **(1)**; semilunar valves **(1)**

17. Blood vessels
Arteries **(1)**

18. Vascular shunting
Reduced blood flow to specific areas of the body is achieved through vascular shunting. **(1)** There is a need for increased blood flow **(1)** to the muscles during exercise.

19. Plasma, platelets and blood cells
White blood cells **(1)**

20. Composition of air
Nitrogen is not used by the body in energy production **(1)**, and it is not made as a by-product of respiration. **(1)**

21. Lung volumes
Vital capacity is the maximum amount of air the lungs can expire after the maximum amount that they can inspire. **(1)**

22. The respiratory system
B Blood transportation **(1)**

23. The alveoli and gas exchange
(a) High concentration **(1)**
(b) The blood in the capillaries has just exchanged gases at the alveoli, so has collected oxygen to take to the muscles. **(1)**

24. Energy and energy sources
1500 metres is too long a race to be able to supply all of the required energy anaerobically **(1)** as anaerobic respiration only produces a limited amount of energy. **(1)** Therefore the 1500-metre runner would tire and slow down as insufficient energy would be available **(1)** compared to the 400-metre runner, who would be able to continue to respire anaerobically throughout their race. **(1)**

25. Short-term effects of exercise on the muscular system
Lactate accumulation is when the level of lactate (a by-product of anaerobic respiration) starts to build up **(1)** in the muscle tissue or blood. **(1)**

26. Short-term effects of exercise on the cardio-respiratory system
(a) Student C **(1)**
(b) Student A **(1)**
(c) Student C **(1)**

27. Lever systems 1
(a) The rower is using a first class lever. **(1)** **(b)** It is a first class lever because the fulcrum is between the load and the effort. **(1)**

28. Lever systems 2
A second class lever operates at the ball of the foot **(1)**, which means it cannot lift the load of the body at high speed **(1)**, making it hard to get a fast start. **(1)**

29. Planes and axes of movement 1

Frontal axis goes from side to side (1); movement will occur in the sagittal plane. (1)

30. Planes and axes of movement 2

Movement occurs in the sagittal plane (1) about the frontal axis. (1)

31. Fitness, health, exercise and performance

D A state of complete emotional, physical and social well-being and not merely the absence of disease and infirmity (1)

32. The relationship between health and fitness

Provided you exercise sensibly, in other words have appropriate rest times between sessions, regular exercise can bring a number of health benefits. (1) These benefits could be physical, social or emotional. (1) For example, weight-bearing exercise can reduce the chance of having osteoporosis later in life. (1)

33. Cardiovascular fitness

Jo and Jus will need to play for 80 minutes without tiring (1) if they are to maintain the quality of their performance throughout the game. (1)

34. Muscular endurance

Muscle endurance is the ability to use voluntary muscles many times without getting tired. (1) Ashley will use the muscular endurance in his arms (1) to allow him to keep working his arm muscles as he rows, allowing him to complete the 3 km without needing to stop and rest. (1)

35. Flexibility

Flexibility will help Sue and Jenny increase their range of movement at the shoulder joint, allowing them to stretch further, (1) for example, for a rebound if the basket is missed. (1)

36. Reaction time

The player may need good reaction time as the ball from the opponent may clip the top of the net, meaning that the original flight of the ball is deflected. (1) Therefore the player will need to make a fast decision to change their direction (1) so they can get to the ball in time before it hits the floor. (1)

37. Power and speed

(i) So they can apply a greater force against the starting blocks. (1): (ii) To get greater height for the jump. (1): (iii) Tennis player serving. (1): (iv) To hit the ball very hard. (1): (v) To make it harder to return so they can win the point. (1)

38. Agility

They would be able to turn quickly at the end of their first run (1) so that they can get a second run, thereby reducing the chance of being run out between wickets as they have spent less time 'turning'. (1)

39. Balance and co-ordination

Golfer: hand (holding club) and eye (1) to allow them to accurately hit the ball in to the hole. (1)
Swimmer: movement of arms and legs at the same time (1) to ensure an efficient stroke, allowing greater generation of power. (1)

40. Body composition and strength

The gymnast needs strength to be able to hold his own body weight in the position (1) and his body composition needs to be a high ratio of muscle to fat to make sure he is not lifting unnecessary weight from excess fat. (1)

41. PARQ and fitness tests

Family history is asked for because if there has been a history of illness, the individual may have a heart condition without knowing. (1) This could put them at risk if exercise is too intense. (1)

42. Cardiovascular fitness tests

Cooper 12-minute run test (1)

43. Strength and flexibility tests

First it would be used to identify Liam's rating, which is below average. (1) The coach would use this as baseline data (1) so that when Liam is retested after training he could see if his flexibility had improved. (1)

44. Agility and speed tests

The Illinois agility run test mimics the dodging movement in a game when swerving in and out of the cones (1), therefore it measures the skill of agility, which is required in a football game to keep possession of the ball. (1) Although strength and flexibility are important to a footballer, they are not as important within the game as it is possible to play well without high levels of grip strength or flexibility. (1)

45. Power and muscular endurance tests

Rowers use repeated contractions of the arm muscles (1), and the one-minute press-up test repeatedly uses the arms so would reflect the activity. (1)

46. Interpreting fitness test results

It is important to analyse and evaluate fitness test results to be able to identify strengths and weaknesses (1) and design appropriate training programmes. (1)

47. Progressive overload

Jamie should measure how long he runs for without a break then increase this amount slightly in the next session. (1) For example, he could run for 20 minutes at the same pace, then try extending this to 21 minutes. (1) He could then continue to gradually increase the time as his body gets used to the new workload so his cardiovascular fitness continues to improve. (1)

48. Specificity

The exercise bike is most likely to be used (1), as it most closely matches the required actions of the sport (1), so when cycling on the bike the cyclist is training the same muscles they will use in their event. (1)

49. Individual needs and overtraining

Overtraining could lead to injury (1) meaning fitness levels may be lost (1) due to not being able to continue with the programme. (1)

50. FITT and reversibility

D How long, hard and often you work, making sure that your training fits the requirements of the activity. (1)

51. Thresholds of training

B (1)

52. Continuous training

Continuous training develops cardiovascular fitness and muscular endurance (1), both of which are required in long-distance running. (1)

53. Fartlek training

You should include sprinting to mirror what you need to do in a game: for example, sprint 20 metres to mimic losing a marker and sprinting for a free ball in a game. (1) You should include jogging to mirror recovery parts in a game after a period of high intensity, such as when you jog back into position. (1)

54. Circuit training

Organise different exercises at stations. **(1)** Work on each station for a set period of time before moving on to the next station. **(1)** Can be fitness-based or skill-based. **(1)**

55. Interval training

Breaks are built into the session. **(1)** The breaks allow recovery. **(1)** The session is made up of repeated sets of reps of work periods and rest periods. **(1)**

56. Plyometric training

Volleyball players need to jump high. **(1)** Plyometrics would develop the power in their legs **(1)** so they would be able to block the ball more easily at the net. **(1)**

57. Weight/resistance training

To increase muscular strength you need fewer repetitions but greater resistance or heavier weights. **(1)** To increase muscular endurance rather than muscular strength you would increase the number of repetitions and reduce the weight lifted, so your muscles get used to working for longer periods of time. **(1)**

58. Fitness classes

Aerobics improves cardiovascular endurance. **(1)** Rugby players need good cardiovascular endurance **(1)** to last the length of the game without losing the quality of their performance. **(1)**

59. Training methods: pros and cons

If something is boring then motivation can be lost. **(1)** This may result in the performer stopping training **(1)** and their performance/fitness levels then dropping. **(1)**

60. The effects and benefits of exercise to the skeletal system

Increased stability of the joint **(1)**; less likely to be injured when being tackled. **(1)**

61. Adaptations to the muscular system

Effect: increased size in muscle. **(1)** Benefit: increased strength. **(1)**

62. Adaptations to the cardiovascular system 1

Good for physical health: for example, there is a reduced chance of coronary heart disease. **(1)**

63. Adaptations to the cardiovascular system 2

Lower resting heart rate **(1)**; increased capillarisation **(1)**; increased number of red blood cells. **(1)**

64. The effects and benefits of exercise to the respiratory system

Means more air can be breathed in **(1)**, therefore there is more oxygen available for energy production. **(1)**

65. Injury prevention 1

Fractured shin: wear shin pads to reduce impact of a blow to the leg. **(1)**
Soft tissue injury: warm up to increase elasticity of muscle. **(1)**

66. Injury prevention 2

Correct clothing **(1)**, warm up **(1)**, correct equipment **(1)**, correct facilities. **(1)**

67. Fractures

Greenstick fracture **(1)** – the bone bends on one side and breaks on the other. **(1)**
Stress fracture **(1)** – a small crack forms in the bone. **(1)**

68. Concussion and dislocation

Example Falling off a bike and banging your head on the road. **(1)** One way to avoid this is to wear a helmet. **(1)**

69. Injuries at joints and soft tissue

Example Hockey: accidentally stepping on the ball and your ankle going over, causing it to twist at the joint. **(1)**

70. Soft tissue injuries and RICE

Theses injuries are often caused by overuse. **(1)** Allow rest and recovery. **(1)**

71. Anabolic steroids

Example Liver damage **(1)**, testicular atrophy **(1)**

72. Beta blockers

They have a calming effect, allowing the heart rate to slow down. **(1)**

73. Diuretics

C Diuretics **(1)**

74. Narcotic analgesics

Narcotic analgesics **(1)**

75. Peptide hormones

EPO increases red blood cell count **(1)**, which means the runner will be able to carry more oxygen **(1)** so they can maintain a good energy supply throughout the race, allowing them to maintain a better pace and run the distance more quickly. **(1)**

76. Stimulants

If a performer has had a long season and is tired **(1)** but needs to be alert for a big event, then they may take stimulants. **(1)**

77. Blood doping

Doping can involve injecting another person's blood into the performer's blood. **(1)** Because the blood is not the performer's own **(1)** they could contract an infection, such as HIV, from the other person's blood. **(1)**

78. Warm up

B The warm up decreases the amount of lactic acid present and therefore reduces the likelihood of muscle soreness after the activity has finished. **(1)**

79. Cool down

after **(1)**, two **(1)**, jogging **(1)**, stretching **(1)**, soreness **(1)**, flexibility. **(1)**

80. Component 1 – Extended answer question 1

Vascular shunting allows the redistribution of blood flow within the body. This means that the body is able to increase blood flow to some areas and decrease it to others. For example, at the start of the football match, through vasoconstriction and vasodilation blood flow is restricted to the digestive system and increased to the active muscles. This is because not so much blood is required for digestion and can be sent to areas where the need is greater, to help with performance.

An increased blood flow to the working muscles means that they will receive more oxygenated blood as oxygen is transported in the blood. With more oxygen, the player will be able to maintain the standard of their play for the duration of the match, for example, continuing to perform effective tackles even late on in the game.

However, there is a drawback. The performer would not be able to eat just before they played or at half time if they were feeling hungry. This could leave them with low energy levels for the second half, therefore they may need to eat a sports bar or something similar that is easy to digest.

Despite the potential problem with not being able to eat, the advantage of the extra oxygen clearly outweighs the chance that someone is hungry, as they can always make sure they get enough to eat on match days in plenty of time before they play.

Also, although the player will not be running all of the time in the game, they still need an elevated supply of oxygen and therefore blood flow as they will need to recover in between bouts of high-intensity exercise. For example, after just chasing a loose ball and passing it on they will need to walk or jog back to position, ready for the next high-intensity demand. Therefore they will need to be able to regulate blood flow to allow for this as well. Without the ability to recover quickly, they would soon stop being effective in the game, for example, they would not be able to run on to through balls or fast breaks.

81. Component 1 – Extended answer question 2

Injury prevention methods are designed to reduce risk. These methods include wearing protective clothing. For example, a boxer will wear gloves on his hands to protect them from bruising or breaking when he strikes his opponent. Without these gloves the boxer would damage his hands, making them too painful to continue to exert force against his opponent, therefore he would have to give up the fight. Amateur boxers also wear head guards to protect the brain; if they didn't have these on and they were struck in the face, the brain could be moved in the skull and this could cause concussion, possibly even brain damage. This type of injury is a threat not just to performance but also to long-term health.

The badminton player doesn't really have protective clothing, but there are other things they need to do to reduce risk of injury. They would warm up and would check the playing area for any spillages so they did not slip on a wet part of the court. If they did, and if they failed to warm up, they would be more likely to pull a muscle, as the muscle fibres would not be pliable enough to cope with the extended range of movement caused by the slip.

Despite the more obvious risk in boxing, if either performer fails to adequately protect themselves against the risks that exist in their activities, they are likely to suffer an injury and therefore be prevented from playing, leading to loss of fitness and reversibility.

82. Improving health

If you design a PEP to promote personal health this means you will have a clear aim about the area of health you want to improve **(1)** and you will design a programme that should, if you follow it, improve that aspect of health. **(1)** For example, if I want to increase the health of my heart and cardiovascular system I would design a PEP that caused me to gradually increase the fitness of this system, improving its health in the process. **(1)**

83. Physical health

Example An example of poor physical health is obesity. **(1)** This would make it harder to run in sporting activities due to additional body fat **(1)**, meaning you could not run very fast or for very long. **(1)**

84. Emotional health

Example If you play sport you will enter competitions **(1)** and this will provide you with an emotional challenge. **(1)** If you are successful, this can make you feel better about yourself, increasing your self-esteem. **(1)**

85. Social health

A social benefit is increased co-operation. **(1)** If you can work with others without arguing (a social benefit), this will increase enjoyment (an emotional benefit). **(1)**

86. Lifestyle choices 1

They will follow a balanced diet **(1)**, eating the right amounts and types of foods. **(1)**

87. Lifestyle choices 2

Example Bronchitis **(1)**; emphysema **(1)**

88. Sedentary lifestyle

Example Driving to work rather than cycling **(1)** can lead to excessive weight gain **(1)** due to not burning calories through inactivity. **(1)**

89. Impact of a sedentary lifestyle on weight

Example 1. Heart disease **(1)**; type 2 diabetes **(1)**
Example 2. By having more body fat than you should you are making your body work harder **(1)**, therefore energy supply will deplete sooner, making it difficult to participate in physical activity. **(1)** This will mean fitness cannot increase, so the individual is less likely to be motivated to sustain involvement in physical activity. **(1)**

90. Diet and energy balance

Example If you don't eat a balanced diet, you could develop a mineral deficiency, such as anaemia from a lack of iron. **(1)**

91. Macronutrients

Example 1. You need to make sure you eat enough carbohydrates to give you the energy you need to exercise. **(1)** 2. The macronutrients are carbohydrates, fats and proteins. **(1)** Fats and carbohydrates are used to provide energy **(1)**, therefore they allow us to be active **(1)**; protein is used for muscle growth and tissue repair, so helps us to remain healthy. **(1)**

92. Micronutrients

B Water, fibre, carbohydrates, fats **(1)**

93. Optimum weight

As bones increase in density, optimum weight will increase. **(1)**

94. Dietary manipulation

They break down muscle tissue due to the explosive nature of their event **(1)** and need to start rebuilding muscle as soon as possible **(1)**, otherwise they would not have the required power to perform in their event. **(1)**

95. Classification of skills 1

An open skill is one that is affected by the environment. **(1)**

96. Classification of skills 2

Because it is difficult to carry out **(1)** and hard to break down the skill into separate phases. **(1)**

97. Massed and distributed practice

Distributed **(1)** as they are young **(1)** and would get bored doing the same thing over and over again. **(1)**

98. Fixed and variable practice

Variable practice **(1)** because passing is an open skill **(1)** and the skill should be practised in different situations so the performer can get used to changes that occur in a game. **(1)**

99. Values of goal setting 1

So you can see if you have achieved your target. **(1)**

100. Values of goal setting 2

Realistic **(1)**

101. Visual and verbal guidance

Visual guidance **(1)**; beginners **(1)**

102. Manual and mechanical guidance

C Performers are supported completing the skill **(1)**

103. Types of feedback

Overall the performer is getting better as they go from 1 to 7 on the success scale. **(1)** It is possible no feedback is given for the first three attempts, but the increase on the fourth and fifth attempts could be due to the introduction of appropriate extrinsic feedback. **(1)** Either feedback is withdrawn for attempts 6 and 7 or it is inappropriate, for example, relying on intrinsic feedback from the performer or the performer had reached their peak without time for further practice. **(1)** Attempts 8 and 9 show a further increase in success; this could be due to the performer developing intrinsic feedback, learning from their own mistakes. **(1)**

104. Mental rehearsal

Mental rehearsal is going though the phases of the run up and jump in his mind. **(1)** This will help the high jumper mentally prepare, focusing on the jump and nothing else. **(1)** This will build his confidence, as he sees himself successfully clearing the bar. **(1)**

105. Socio-economic groups

Managerial/professional have the highest participation rates **(1)**; in fact, the percentages increase with socio-economic group **(1)**, the lowest group participating the least. **(1)** The closest levels of participation are between the third and fourth categories of socio-economic group. **(1)**

106. Gender and age groups

The trend shows a rise in female participation between October 2011 and 2012. **(1)**

107. Ethnicity and disability groups

Lack of access **(1)** as there might not be any clubs in the area. **(1)**

108. Commercialisation, the media and sport

Because they get huge audiences **(1)** therefore increasing the number of people worldwide that will see their product and want to buy or use it. **(1)**

109. The advantages of commercialisation

Their product will be associated with the best in the sport **(1)**, therefore fans will think the product is good and want to buy it. **(1)**

110. The disadvantages of commercialisation

The company is associated with cheating **(1)** therefore the product is no longer as popular **(1)** and sales will go down. **(1)**

111. Sporting behaviour

Sportsmanship **(1)**

112. Deviance in sport

Example An elite performer might take PEDs to win **(1)** and therefore get better sponsorship deals. **(1)**

113. Component 2 – Extended answer question 1

When performers exercise they need to ensure they have enough energy to work at a high level for the duration of their activity. They also need to make sure they have enough protein to repair any muscle damage or to build larger muscles.

Energy can come from fats or carbohydrates. Sometimes when performers lose, it is due to a lack of energy, so they try to find ways to alter their diet to give them more energy. Carbohydrate loading is when a performer manipulates their diet by decreasing training intensity and increasing carbohydrate intake 1 to 4 days before an event. They do this to maximise their carbohydrate stores for energy. This is due to the increase in glycogen in the muscle, meaning they can perform at a high quality for longer.

Timing of protein intake is when performers take in extra protein as soon as possible after their activity. They do this in addition to the required rest and recovery needed for muscle growth and repair, to increase protein synthesis to get the muscle to grow faster and bigger so they can generate more power. Endurance athletes do need some power for pace in the race, for example, to accelerate. However, they wouldn't want bulky muscles, as this would mean more weight to carry and could potentially slow them down.

Of the two techniques, therefore, carbohydrate loading is the most beneficial strategy for endurance athletes. It means the cyclist will increase the energy stores for during the race so they can delay muscle fatigue, allowing them to work harder for longer to last the distance of their race. The timing of protein intake would be more relevant for power athletes who need to build muscle, for example, sprinters or weightlifters.

114. Component 2 – Extended answer question 2

There are different types of guidance: visual, verbal, manual and mechanical.

Visual guidance is where the performer is shown the skill being completed correctly so that they can see how it should look and then copy it. Frankie's coach could demonstrate the back somersault or ask someone else who was good at them to demonstrate. This type of guidance is very useful with beginners as this helps them to develop a mental image of the skill they need to perform.

Verbal guidance is when the coach gives teaching points. For example, they may shout 'hips forward and up' to remind Frankie about that part of the technique. However, this is only any good if Frankie knows what this means. As he is a beginner at this skill, he is unlikely to understand and therefore will not do the technique correctly, which is likely to result in injury.

To help avoid injury the coach could use either manual or mechanical guidance. In manual guidance the coach would physically support Frankie to complete the move. This would probably be via a harness so that, if Frankie does the skill incorrectly, the coach can stop Frankie crashing to the trampoline. This reduces the chance of injury and will increase Frankie's confidence before attempting without support. Even though this would be the best method, the coach needs to be careful not to let Frankie become too reliant on it. If he does, it will be difficult psychologically for Frankie to attempt the move without the harness.

Preparing for your exam

Checklist for exam day

- ✓ Eat well
- ✓ Get there early

Remember:

- ✓ Pens (yes, more than one. They always run out on exam day!)
- ✓ Pencil – for drawing diagrams or graphs
- ✓ Ruler
- ✓ Eraser
- ✓ Write neatly
- ✓ Spell as well as you can. If in doubt sound it out and spell the word as it sounds.

Go for your own personal gold!

Preparing for your PE exam is the same as preparing for any event. So train for it!

Practice

The more you practise (revise), the more you will understand. The more you train, the better your performance.

Pace yourself

You need to peak at the right time, so plan your revision. You can still do other things if you are organised. Put the topics in your diary and stick to the plan.

Don't stay up late the night before your exam: you want to be at your best for your 'event'.

Good luck and see you on the podium!

Notes

Notes